AF317023

OUT *of the* WHIRLWIND

PRAISE FOR
OUT OF THE WHIRLWIND

In prose as polished as the surface of the life portrayed here, Longstreth sketches a moving portrait of a man wholly of his mid-century era. A white, Ivy-league trained lawyer living what appears to be a charmed life, with wife and child, on the upper East side of Manhattan—who is in reality tormented, hiding his homosexual longings in a closet of privilege. Longstreth elegantly captures the poignancy of a short-lived personal triumph, when Adam Zopher Hudson finally breaks out, falls in love and builds a new life with a man--cut tragically short by AIDS.

–Dominique Browning, Writer, Editor,
Director of Moms Clean Air Force

Bevis Longstreth's *Out of the Whirlwind* memorably evokes the privileged worlds of elite colleges and law firms, New York of the 60s, 70s, and 80s, and fathers who name their sailboats after the daughters they never had, and imagines what it must've been like for one closeted young man to negotiate those spaces without blowing up his place in them. The novel asks not only where we belong, but where we *want* to belong, and at its heart is the story of an aspirational father, the son who wants to please him, and the power they each hold over the other.

–Karen Shepard, author, most recently, *Kiss Me Sometime*

Fearless as ever, Bevis Longstreth has now tackled one of the most complex subjects in contemporary life. This is his strongest novel yet.

–Frances Taliaferro, Book Critic and
Retired Teacher, Brearley School

"The hero of *Out of the Whirlwind*, Bevis Longstreth's latest novel, is pushed along life's path by his desire to please a domineering father -- until an unexpected love enters his life. Not only are the characters well drawn but the settings -- from prep school to law firm -- take the reader into the world which first confines him and then becomes a place where he can merge laws and love. "

–Susan Carey, Book Critic and Editor

Out of the Whirlwind is set in a world the author knows well, white shoe New York corporate law firms and the Ivy League schools whose products populate them. Its protagonist comes of age in mid-century America, scales the highest of academic and professional heights and in mid-life comes to terms with a deeply conflicted identity. Looming over all is his controlling father, an unescapable but ultimately unknowable figure. The story is absorbing and, despite its grim end, is told with great wit and pitch-perfect dialogue worthy of John O'Hara.

–Thomas M. Kelly, Partner, Debevoise & Plimpton

Bevis Longstreth's new novel, *Out of the Whirlwind*, takes its title from the Book of Job. It is a tale of Adam, a male whose youth was consumed with ambiguous sexuality, and whose life, shortened by AIDS contracted in the time of gay emancipation, was one of turmoil, triumph and tragedy. In taking on one of contemporary society's major dilemmas, its boldness and nuanced understanding in depicting the protagonist and those around him achieve an authenticity highly rewarding to readers.

–Tim Wirth, Former U.S. Senator for Colorado.

Bevis Longstreth has departed from his use of the novel to examine historical events to write a sensitive examination of the life of a brilliant lawyer shaped by an overbearing father, his struggles to come to terms with his sexuality, the lies and pain of being closeted in New York in the time of AIDS, and the ultimate satisfaction that comes from acceptance and honesty. To a retired partner of a major law firm, the arc of Adam Hudson's life and career rings true.

–Bruce D. Haims, Retired Partner, Debevoise & Plimpton

Yet again, in *Out of the Whirlwind*, Bevis Longstreth has imaginatively created a compelling life story in a meticulously observed and described setting. His previous novels included the vivid telling of the lives of two extraordinary women in Central Asia some 400 years before the Christian era. His latest work portrays a life taking place in educational, professional, and cultural worlds that Longstreth knows first-hand, and describes with precision and insight. The result is deeply moving and convincing.

–Thomas H. Wright, Retired General
Counsel, Princeton University

Out of the Whirlwind
Copyright © 2023 by Bevis Longstreth
Honeycomb Publishers

First Edition 2023

Cover painting by Noah Saterstrom
Book jacket design and interior formatting by
Golden Ratio Book Design

This is a work of fiction. All of the characters, organizations, and events portrayed in this novel either are products of the author's imagination or are used fictitiously.

ISBN 979-8-218-10396-5 Hardcover
ISBN 979-8-218-10397-2 Ebook

Printed in the United States of America

OUT *of the* WHIRLWIND

Bevis Longstreth

HONEYCOMB
PUBLISHERS

New York, New York

❧ 1 ❧

1989

"Bernie, can you hear me? Water. Please. And my glasses."

Bernie appeared at Adam's bedside, having heard the cry from their study, where he was deep into a novel.

"What do you need?"

Sheepishly, Adam repeated his request. Bernie picked the glasses off the floor and filled Adam's bedside cup with water from the pitcher on the table.

As involuntary as his tears, the source of this irritant he sought by examining what was going on between those toes.

"Bernie, I can't go on this way. So fucking helpless."

"Adam Zopher Hudson, the Spartan. We do this, again and again. You're scared of dependence like a cat fears water. I know your old man grew up in Montana, but, I mean, so what. Did he teach you to run away from love? Come on Adam, let me in—where my help won't bring on this conflict."

He took Adam's hand.

"Do you think I have that place?"

"I know you do. I first saw it, the night we met on the way out of that bathhouse. Remember? Not just that. Over beers, we talked. You showed me that night, in your face, by your voice, a loneliness. And a need and capacity for love. So, yes, you've been there, but the way's hardscrabble; not well marked."

From 180 pounds of muscle, Adam had shrunk to 160 pounds of weakness, afflicted with intractable diarrhea, neuropathy and red scaly lesions on his torso and, in a cruel twist, that procuring cause, his penis. His still beautiful face, though gaunt, had been spared, with its chiseled Celtic nose, etched cheekbones and deep-set cornflower eyes. Adam had feared a diagnosis and had postponed seeking one many times before Bernie was able to coax him into booking a doctor's appointment, late last year, some 12 months after the symptoms first appeared. By that time, he felt hopeless.

Adam remembered being given the diagnostic report in January. The doctor had gone over it with him, but he hadn't taken in the reality of the doctor's words. Because he didn't need to. Returning to their apartment, he'd handed the paper to Bernie.

"I knew," Adam said, "It's over now, all but the grieving. And the tiding up."

Adam had swabbed his brain of all save anger. He had shivered; he had cried; he had struggled to accept a verdict that he thought grossly unfair—an unjust death sentence.

Adam had been true to Bernard Kraus since they'd met six years earlier, literally bumping into one another, while exiting the Flamingo bathhouse one night in April of 1983. Adam kept the relationship a secret from his wife and son for the next two years. Adam and Bernie knew as much about the plague as anyone. They used condoms and took other precautions designed to protect them. In theory, they also knew of the shockingly long asymptomatic carrier state. But in practice, not unlike a reckless driver convinced he was immune to risk, it proved impossible for either of them to imagine they could be affected. "I know," Adam said to Bernie soon after they fell in love: "Either of us could have gotten HIV during our time in the bathhouses and then incubated for a few years. Possible but highly unlikely."

Bernie agreed. "We'll cross that bridge when we come to it. Our time in the bathhouses was brief. Not to worry."

"It's unfair," Bernie whispered, releasing Adam. "It's unfair. Get out of bed, come into the kitchen, I have some coffee brewing.

Adam's rage found only himself to target. Bernie was right. My life, not perfect in every dimension, he thought as they sat at the table while Bernie brought two cups of coffee. But Adam believed his had been a life of meaning and contribution—to his family, to Liz and George, to his law practice and to the society in which he had grown and thrived. He gave back through charities in board service rendered and cash contributed.

Raised in a Christian home, at some point in his high school years, Adam had rejected the magical claims on which that religion rested. Still, he could imagine what a God might look like, if there were one. He would not be given to unfairness. He would reward, not punish, those who lived a good life. While in the doctor's office awaiting the diagnosis, he had returned to the Book of Job, about whom, as an undergraduate, he had written an essay, leveraging William Blake's illustrations. The professor thought it a superior bit of analysis, which led Adam to develop an enduring sympathy for Job. Now, it felt as if he were walking in that ancient man's shoes.

> Thou knowest that I am not wicked;
>> and there is none that can deliver out of thine hand.
> Thine hands have made me and fashioned me together
>> round about;
>> yet thou dost destroy me.

They were sitting at the kitchen table. Adam seized Bernie's hands and exclaimed, "I don't deserve it. A good life ought not end in AIDS."

"No life should end that way. But we've been around enough to know there's no fairness to life, no reciprocity, no divine Sherpa who says, if you do this, then that will follow. Pray and your wish will be answered. We know it just *don't* work that way. I feel your complaint. I share it. I understand the injustice. Job does come to mind. I remember seeing MacLeish's *J.B.* on Broadway. Around '59."

Adam stood to scratch some of the lesions on his arms and chest.

"Damn these itches. The MacLeish play. I had totally forgotten it. You know, MacLeish went to Harvard Law, but he only practiced for three years, at a Boston law firm. Who knows, perhaps he was driven into law school by an insistent father."

"Yeah, it happens."

"MacLeish was in a secret club there. The Choate. Damn it Bernie, you're distracting me. I was trying to rage at someone and now we're sitting here, talking calmly about MacLeish and Job. Okay, let the thoughts flow. Ever since college I've loved Blake's illustrations of the Book of Job, looking at them while pondering the reality—or not—of God. My favorite is Plate ... Can't remember the number. But here's what it depicts:

'Then the Lord answered Job out of the whirlwind.'"

Adam sat down, aware that his scratching had only irritated his skin more.

As for AIDS, that Lord is AWOL," Bernie said, shaking his head.

"That's not what the homophobes say. They say—indeed, they believe—it is God's punishment for the sin of homosexuality, making Job's story inapposite, because he'd done nothing that deserved punishment."

"And neither have you!" Bernie squeezed Adam's hands. "Yes to your outrage, yes to fathomless unfairness. But it's not, necessarily, a death sentence. You've got a life yet to live, buddy. And I'm planning on being around to share it. So let's suck it up, both of us. Exhale. Let's plan next steps."

"Fuck it, Bernie. Don't deny me the right to rage."

"No, I'm just trying to limit you," he said, smiling. "You know, Adam, we have a lot in common. The only child thing. Growing up, an abandoned belief in God. And, now, together—in love and life. And look, we must be happy. Anyway we can."

"We didn't share Brooklyn, thank the heavens. You're turning spiritual. It drops my rage like a spent dick."

"Ha! You know what comes to mind? Growing up a Jew with atheistic tendencies, I questioned our Rabbi about the existence of Yahweh. He told me a story I found, literally, wonderful. The four Hebrew letters are YHWH. He said they stand for 'The Lord.' One says 'Yahweh' with deep breaths in and out, 'Yah' to fill the lungs and 'weh' to empty them. In other words 'breath' is the meaning of God. I got it and held on, from the moment I heard the Rabbi's tale. It was a meaning of God to my liking, and I bet to yours too. Something even atheists could embrace."

"Great story. Jews are deep. You remind me of that guy in *Daniel Deronda*, remember, the brother of the girl Daniel saves from drowning, the one dying of consumption. The girl he marries."

"Mordecai. Great book. I'll take his depth, but not the consumption, thank you very much."

Bernie stood to get the coffee pot and poured its remains in their cups. Sitting down, he said: "Have you thought about telling your parents? They need to know."

"You don't kid around, Jocko. Go right for the jugular. Father! You know, when I called Liz to give her the diagnosis, and asked her to tell George, she asked me the same thing. But even she backed away from advising me to tell my father."

Adam drifted back to the time when he and Liz were separating, He had tried to explain to his father how he came to the point of not being able to take the pretense and falsity any more.

"There was so much to tell him, to have him understand, even if he couldn't fully accept it, having a gay son—his only child. But he had refused to listen. He turned away, as if I were infected. He closed his ears. Before he turned, I saw, or imagined, Father's face riddled with conflicting emotions, sadness and shame, anger and frustration, even a hint of failure. But failure was something beyond all things, he couldn't abide. Wright Alexander Hudson. Named with purpose."

"I know it's hard. Worse than stepping up to the plate after the pitcher has struck you out a couple of times. But now it's different. Call him up. Book a time to see him. Try again to reach him. Somewhere in that soul of his there's something like understanding and love. He's not a monster. It's got to be there. Go find it. And if you can't, it will be not for lack of trying. Either way, you'll feel better for not having given up."

Adam felt wrung out and exhausted by Bernie's compelling logic. He stared down into his half-drained coffee cup, as if seeking an answer in the blackness. Finally, looking at Bernie, he said, "Okay, I guess you're right. Hand me the phone. I'll call him."

The appointment was made. At 3 tomorrow Adam would be at his father's Columbia Law School office.

Adam arrived on time and knocked on the door. Professor Hudson opened it, looked Adam over and, unable to conceal the shock, extended his hand. Adam had widened his arms to embrace his father, but seeing the hand outstretched, and sensing his father's flinch, he dropped his arms and gripped the hand instead. To Adam the office air was heavy. He was edgy.

"Good to see you, son. Take a seat."

The Professor was a handsome man in his early sixties, with well attended white hair, deep-set dark brown eyes, an aquiline nose more suggestive of a merlin than an eagle, and the upright stature of a Marine Corps Sergeant Major. His eyes were special. They were close set and partially covered by lids that angled sharply down from the bridge of his nose, creating a highly focused and perpetually worried look that was only dispersed with laughter. He was not overly tall at six feet. But long ago he had adjusted the chair behind his desk so that even the tallest student who might be summoned to his office could not sit with head higher than his own. Among his colleagues on the Columbia faculty, he was respected for his intellect and teaching skills but found by many to be too remote, stiff and tightly contained to embrace warmly as a friend. Perhaps the absence of friends among his colleagues was due, in large measure, to his absolute unwillingness to share anything about himself, beyond his opinions of the news of the day. In a word he was too private to befriend.

Adam hadn't seen, or even been in touch with, his father for several years, since his painful, vastly unsuccessful effort to explain why he and Liz were separating.

"So, Father, what news? How go things Columbian?" Hearing himself, Adam thought: pathetic.

"Well, son …" His father stopped. "You've lost a lot of weight. Dieting?" Wright appeared nervous, not sure what had happened to his stolid offspring. Adam was not sure whether his question was intended as a joke or something else.

"So, what brings you here? More, I suppose, than to hear a new limerick," Wright said, chuckling nervously. "Remember how you were always picking my pocket for the latest limerick I'd heard on campus. In fact, I have a new one, if you'd like." Without a pause, Wright recited:

> There was a young lady of Lynn,
>
> Who was so uncommonly thin
>
> That when she essayed
>
> To drink lemonade
>
> She slipped through the straw and fell in.

"That's new to me. But, let me get to the point." Adam's voice dropped almost to a whisper.

"I've been diagnosed with AIDS." Adam looked hard into his father's eyes. Wright turned away, staring out the window.

"I wanted you to hear this from me. I hoped it might allow us to … to talk."

"Could the diagnosis be wrong? You don't look well. Are you still living with that man, what's his name—Bernard? Is he positive too?" Wright swung his chair around to face his son. His face had become a map of agonies. He was slumped in his chair—enough to bring his head level with Adam's.

"Yes, I live with Bernie. And no, he's not positive."

"I knew it would come to this. I put it to you, son, was sex worth dying for?"

Adam flinched, feeling the blow as a fighter hit hard.

Wright had, again, swung his chair around, his back to his son, his face to the window. Even now, under these life-changing circumstances, Wright was going to remain the father he had grown up with.

"I'm not dead yet, Father. And my love for Bernie is far beyond sex. From day one I've done your bidding. Always trying to make you proud and gain your approval. I went from Princeton to Harvard Law, as directed. I made the Law Review, was elected its President. Then, I put aside my desire to clerk for Brennan in favor of your insistent voice for Stewart. Then rapid success as a partner at Bundy. I married the one you favored. None of it was enough."

Looking across the desk, he saw only his father's back. He felt defiant.

"I'm sorry I'm a disappointment. Sorrier still for your impossibly high, and highly conventional, expectations for me."

Wright turned back to face his son.

"Oh, please. Don't be such a child. There have been disappointments, to be sure. When you were a teenager, we faced the usual problem of how your character should be developed. You will remember. We offered you an option: a paper route or learning to play the piano. Either we imagined would build character. You chose the piano. But you didn't have the talent. Your competitor at school, Billy Waite, had the ability to become a concert pianist. But you didn't, and your little recital was an embarrassment to us, and to you too, I recall. It was then we knew you might sometimes fall short. Although often, I recall—being honest about it—you exceeded our expectations. There have been, I agree, many accomplishments, ones that made us proud. That amazing memory we helped you develop, early on. But, as for doing my bidding, we had discussed what name you'd choose for your son. I thought we'd settled on Wright, with a different middle name from mine, of course. But you chose George without so much as an explanation. That hurt. And now this. What you've done to us, and to Liz and your son—why I find it outside all limits; simply unimaginable." Wright's expression had developed into self-endearing pout, his fists clenched. They locked eyes for one brief moment of tension; then each looked away.

Adam rose from his chair and turned to go, feeling his anger make room for a bone-deep sadness. He knew some of what his father said was true. The damage done to Liz and George was not only real but enduring, and no pain or apology on his part could erase it. But for Adam these truths could not excuse the rest. It was selfish, and, within any fair meaning of parenting, un-fatherly. These thoughts smoldered in his head, but, as one might suppress a fire by covering it, Adam denied himself the kind of release that his father so easily found with his.

"This was not—Father—the talk I had hoped for. Or expected. I can see I embarrass you. I'll let it go at that."

Wright watched his son's retreat with sadness. How, he wondered, could a son of such promise disappoint so thoroughly all those who had supported him, who, like his parents, had enabled him to achieve that promise. Wright saw only bitter harvest.

Adam left the office crushed by his father's inability to cope with his son's homosexuality, much less the sentence AIDS had marked him with. He imagined the effects on his father's idea of accomplishment as a parent, the sense of failure that might have been generated. He crossed Amsterdam Avenue to enter Low Plaza and sat down on the rain-washed steps, now bright in a warm sun, leading to Columbia's massive library.

With a wry smile faintly visible across his face, he mused over the name of the place he chose to sit. And, then, tumbling thoughts. There was a time, he recalled, when he rejoiced in being with his father. And his father in being with him. Learning to sail, for example. When he was eleven, and just strong enough to be given the tiller, his father had taught him to sail, how to point the craft upwind till the jib lost the tiniest particle of air and then to back off a touch, and feel the craft respond, gaining in purpose, cutting through the oncoming waves. Adam remembered his father's instructions, carefully given, even gently, when Adam veered off course, and his father's radiant smile when Adam sailed well, according to instructions.

Wright taught Adam the basics, how to come about, to jibe, to round a marker, be it black can or red nun, and how to drop the jib and replace it with the spinnaker, grabbing the spinnaker sheets while dashing astern to the tiller, watching as the wind caught the multi-colored sail, bellying it out to pull the craft, racing forward. And Adam knew his father was a good teacher.

Adam remembered so much about the wind. Father always claimed it never came unsummoned. Or all at once, in a whoosh. You felt it as a chill on the skin, faintly, and then stronger, across the cheek and down the neck. It built and, almost in lock-step, the craft moved and you with it, fairly shivering with excitement.

His thoughts waded even further upstream, to an eight-year old proudly presented by his father to a Sunday luncheon party to recite the Gettysburg Address. Looking across the quad, he felt again his nervousness, compounded by a tiny tremor in his father's voice as he introduced Adam and the performance he was about to render. How his own voice, cautious at first, gained strength as he realized that Lincoln's words would flow easily from memory, words mastered through many practice runs supervised by an anxious parent. What he remembered most powerfully was his father's pleasure in his son's success, in the audience's enthusiasm, and his own happiness in having rewarded his father this way.

Sitting on the Low Steps, he had other thoughts, ones from the painful side of the ledger. The fact that Father never kissed him, or from about seven on never even hugged him. Had never said he loved Adam. These recessed feelings were like wounds left open to fester. Adam was surprised to realize that, never, not even once, had he broached these matters with either parent.

Casting his mind back to the beginning, he wondered what had gone wrong. When and how, so terribly wrong? Why did the ship slip its mooring? It was a question he could not answer, at least not without defending himself and placing the blame on some deep grooves of intolerance etched over time in his father's head. He tried to imagine Wright's father's influence on Wright, and the influence of others as well, and saw in this jumble of ideas the impossibility of unbraiding the many strands that, woven together, made the man in full who was Wright Alexander Hudson. With a wry smile, he acknowledged that it was his strong memory of the past that heightened the pain of the present.

1988

The telephone rang. Bernie answered.

"It's for you. Byard Scott, the Conductor. He with the faux British accent."

Byard asked Adam to join him for lunch the next day, and they agreed on meeting at The Empire, a club where Byard was a member.

"I wonder what he wants me for. He said he sought my judgment on some programming ideas."

"Interesting. The Empire's that pretentious outfit in midtown, on the West Side. It was supposed to be for writers and artists. I've heard that lawyers had almost taken over the joint. Just the place for your buddy Scott.

Byard Scott was the Music Director of the West Side Community Chorale, a first-rate amateur chorus that Adam had rejoined after parting with Liz and coming out to his closest colleagues at Bundy, Rogers & Freund. He had sung with WSCC upon starting his career at Bundy, but lasted only one season because demands of the law firm and on the home front left too little time for such a serious avocation.

Adam met Byard in the lobby of The Empire, which led to grand stairs dividing at the first level to become twin stairs to a large reception room, adjoining two other large rooms. The dining rooms and library were on the third floor.

Adam inhaled the old-world air about the place, which Byard said had been designed by the famed architectural trio, McKim, Mead & White. It had the eloquent and dusty feel of age, and yet was scrubbed clean. The staff greeted members by name, pegging them in and out on a peg board in the lobby. Guests were steered to a visitor's log, where, in Adam's case, he was signed in by Byard. "It's not just a formality. They limit a guest to one visit per month. Let's take the elevator." Adam surmised that Byard wanted him to notice that the elevator was illuminated by a light hung overhead, enclosed in an umbrella of beautiful, turn-of-the-century wrought-iron decoration.

From his first rehearsal with the West Side Community Chorale, Adam had identified its conductor as a homosexual. He was thin and wiry. Penetrating eyes below deeply lined brow. A nose too small to be easily tweaked and slight lips that were easily overlooked. A weak chin disappearing into his slim neck. His voice was high pitched and perhaps intended to be seductive. And then there was the clothing, the British façade, the way he waved his hands, the *je ne sais quoi*, all of it pointed to this conclusion. It was only those deep-set eyes that commanded attention. But they were enough, together with an electric energy, to lure and hold a 60 voice chorus.

Adam didn't know how uncloseted Byard might be, and for that reason, as well as a natural shyness, he avoided trying to connect.

After scribbling down their lunch orders, Byard turned to the chorus, asking Adam if he would be willing to help in developing a program for the next year's spring concert, scheduled in late May of 1989.

Adam said "Of course I'm willing. But I bring no particular expertise to the table. What theme do you have in mind?"

"The theme for this concert is AIDS. I am asking you to help because I know a bit of your background, that you are out of the closet, and out of a marriage and have had a partner for some time. I hoped your experience would help in shaping the program."

Caught unaware, Adam struggled to frame a response. Despite the growing symptomatic evidence, he hadn't seen a doctor, refusing to accept the story his body was telling, or the urgings of Bernie to get checked out. Could Byard know something even he didn't? No, no need for panic. "You're gay too, right?"

"It's why this idea is so important to me. I have friends—good friends—who have been killed by AIDS. A concert devoted to this theme seemed to me a way of deepening understanding and even helping the cause in some melodic way. And remembering those friends."

"I'm delighted to help."

"Splendid! Now, the first challenge is a title for the concert."

"If you will allow me, how about *Death in the Time of AIDS*."

"That's a start. But a bit depressing. How about adding 'Life'? *Life and Death in the Time of AIDS*."

"Much better, especially if you want to give the program some uplift. Do you have some music in mind?"

"Well, one piece by William Schuman is on my A list. It puts to music poems on the theme of death by Walt Whitman: 'The Last Invocation' and 'The Unknown Region.' Both from 'Leaves of Grass.' I am hoping you'll come up with more."

Dessert and coffee had been served, together with an elevated serving tray covered with macaroons.

"I'll have to do some research. Two of my favorite poems are Dylan Thomas's 'Fern Hill' and Edna St. Vincent Millay's 'God's World.' The poems would be right for this program, but I don't know if anyone has set them. Do you?"

"Try these macaroons. A club specialty. I think 'Fern Hill' was set by John Corigliano. A good piece."

"Yes, you recall the last lines: 'Oh as I was young and easy in the mercy of his means, time held me green and dying though I sang in my chains like the sea.' It will work well with your program."

"I don't know *God's World*. Let's go into the library and look it up. I love Millay's poems too. Perhaps we could commission a piece set to something by her."

The library had the musty feeling of a great number of unused books, encased in well preserved dark wood cases. On the central table in the room were books recently written by the club's members. The Empire's famously helpful librarian took less than five minutes to hand over the poem.

Adam began to catch Byard's character. Quiet confidence, a sure sense that anything he wanted to accomplish could be accomplished—end of story. What a great approach to conducting, he thought. He asked Byard if he had lived in the UK.

"Never did. You must be connecting that idea with my tiny, off-on British accent. I admire the British. I see no shame in copying what I admire."

They examined the poem, until then unfamiliar to Byard:

O world, I cannot hold thee close enough!

Thy winds, thy wide grey skies!

Thy mists, that roll and rise!

Thy woods, this autumn day, that ache and sag

And all but cry with colour! That gaunt crag

To crush! To lift the lean of that black bluff!

World, World, I cannot get thee close enough!

Long have I known a glory in it all'

But never knew I this:

Here such a passion is

As stretcheth me apart,—Lord, I do fear

Thou'st made the world too beautiful this year;

My soul is all but out of me,—let fall

No burning leaf; prithee, let no bird call.

Byard instantly embraced the poem. By his third reading he was plotting some way to entice a composer to set the lines to music. He could allow time, almost a year before the concert.

"This poem works. It's on message. Beyond that, it's got rhythm. All we need are the notes. I'm going to try Charles Williamson. He's got reasons to find this program appealing. You know, Millay must have been a roguish vagabond."

"Yes, with upper-class roots and all-embracing sexuality. She owned an island in Maine. I've sailed there. I'm told she used the island for solitude, where she could escape and dry out after weeks of mad gaiety in New York City's night life. Apparently, the candle she put into that famous poem, about burning at both ends, and not lasting the night, was a metaphor for her own life. She died young."

They parted with Adam promising to work on ideas. For his part, Byard said he would line up Williamson for a commission and figure out some way to get gay leaders like Larry Kramer, Edmund White and Randy Shilts to the concert. And then he was off, walking fast toward 5ᵗʰ Avenue with a wave of the hand, toss of the head and the believable claim, voiced in his high-pitched way, loudly enough for Adam to hear standing on the steps of the Empire: "This concert's shaping up bloody well!"

By late August, 1988, Adam was ready to suggest some choral pieces to Byard. The attraction of choral singing had waxed for Adam to the point where he looked forward to rehearsals more than his practice at Bundy, and perhaps equal to his life with Bernie. Even more than cooking.

Again, Byard took Adam to lunch at the Empire. The "no papers" rule at table dictated that they postpone the choral program for the AIDS concert until after lunch, when they could repair to a couple of over-stuffed leather chairs in a corner on the second floor. Outside, the weather was uncommonly hot and humid, but the thick walls of the Empire combined with mild air conditioning to make the room felicitous for serious talk.

"So, what have you come up with?" Byard asked.

"I have three suggestions that deal more or less directly with death. Then, thinking about those, I sought balance in songs that deal with the glories of life. I have three for you to consider. By the way, what happened to the idea of commissioning Millay's poem."

"On that front, no luck yet. If what you've got works out, we won't need much more. Give me your ideas. Wait, first some more coffee."

A waiter had just placed a pot and two cups on the table beside their chairs.

"My first idea is the poem by Thomas Nashe, 'In Time of Pestilence,' written in 1593 and set to music by Ned Rorem in 1973. Moving, powerful and relevant to our new wave of disease."

"Perfect. I am remiss. I don't know the piece. But I know Rorem. Can't wait to hear it. Go on."

The other two are *Crossing the Bar* by Charles Ives, setting the poem by Tennyson, and *Let Down the Bars, O Death* by Samuel Barber, setting the poem by Emily Dickenson."

"Done. I know them both and would love to have the chorus sing them. You're batting a thousand. Who's up next?"

Adam couldn't help admiring Byard. For his petulant impatience, his false innocence, his faux accent and a self-parodying love of baseball metaphor, which he deployed constantly in rehearsals, coming up with new and sometimes strange analogies just when the whole chorus thought his repertoire was exhausted. As an athlete he must have been pathetic.

"Okay, here's the pitch. I don't know how to rank them, but I offer three to consider. The poems are among my favorite few. First might come *Pied Beauty* by Thomas Beveridge, setting the poem by Gerard Manley Hopkins. For men's voices. Then *Fern Hill* by John Corigliano, setting the poem by Dylan Thomas. And finally, *Simple Gifts* from Appalachian Spring by Arron Copland, setting the Shaker poem."

"These are great suggestions. I know them all. The common theme is nature, its change, the seasons as an endless procession of life begetting death begetting life, and, especially in Thomas, the rapturous, yet brief life we can hope for. You've pitched a no hitter."

"Really? Aren't you being hasty? I mean, what are your ideas?"

"Hasty is what I practice. Your ideas trump mine. It's done. Our program is complete."

With the music set, rehearsals turned with gleeful intensity to the selected pieces. The members of the chorus fairly shouted out their enthusiasm for both the theme of the May Concert and the music. Adam had never, even with the Nassoons at Princeton, experienced such energy, collectively pulsing within the cocoon that Byard had woven to capture the singers and inspire them.

❧ 3 ❧

1985

It was September 20, 1985, their 23st wedding anniversary. An event they tried to honor each year, renewing their vows, as if it were possible for them not to hold tight, but often in a humorous vein, tongue in cheek. Liz had shopped early. They planned on a quiet celebration. Their son, George, a sophomore at Cornell, wouldn't be home until Thanksgiving. Liz was in the kitchen, rubbing Adam's favorite cut of steak with the garlic he craved, when the telephone rang. She looked at the clock and knew it was Adam, calling to say he was "stuck at work, don't know how long I'll be, best postpone the celebration, don't wait up, love you."

How many times had this been rehearsed? But on our wedding anniversary, Liz questioned, anger beginning to rise in her throat. Early in their marriage, Adam had trained her to know his work came first, and she had long accepted this fact. Resigned, she knew it was about two decades too late to change priorities.

He slid into bed without waking her. It was just past 3. He had showered in the downstairs bathroom. At 7 they rolled out of bed together, shared the bathroom and got some cereal, fruit and coffee in the kitchen.

"When did you get home?"

"Not till two. Unexpectedly difficult piece of drafting, and a deadline today."

"What poor associate were you torturing last night?"

"All alone. Not even Ellen, the faithful one. She had to break off at 8—family issue. Lucky I can type. How was your evening? I know. Our anniversary. I can smell the steak. We'll pick another evening to celebrate. Okay?" He extended his hand across the kitchen table, and she met it with hers halfway. She started to cry, and then, she laughed.

"Want to know something funny? I lathered the steak with the garlic you lust after, and I hate, and then I had to eat it."

Adam winced as he reached for her other hand.

"Funny, yes, but not fun. Sorry about last night. Really sorry. But, you know that line about the jealous mistress. Got to run back to her right now, alas. Bye Babe, hope to finish the draft by lunch. Have a good one!"

He swung around the table, bent over and kissed her on her neck. Then, grabbing his briefcase, quick as lightning, he was out the door, headed for the Lexington Avenue Subway.

Liz started to clean up the kitchen. Looking at the dishwasher, she was dismayed to remember it was full and had been run. Feeling empty, she sat again. It was not about the dishes needing to be removed before she could fill it again. The regularity of Adam's late night routine had long depressed her. Resolving soon to try again, and harder, to have the long delayed talk about their marriage that Adam had repeatedly, with many clever excuses, found a way to duck, she rose and resumed cleaning up the kitchen. The talk would be hard, she knew. Long ago, his pattern had been imposed on their lives, and she had gone along. Now she would try to insist on more of a partnership. One, she would argue, at least equal to Adam's partnership with colleagues in the firm. She would explain that she was a jealous mistress too, a wife too often demoted to backup, the supporting role to the breadwinner in the family.

She remembered planning to do a load of laundry. She still ironed his shirts, although she didn't have to, finding it a mindless yet skillful exercise that allowed her brain to empty and recharge. The hamper was full, with Adam's day-old shirt on top of the heap. Emptying his shirt pocket, she found, as often was the case, the 3 by 5 card on which Ellen had typed out the day's appointments.

But there was also a scrap of paper with a telephone number, the number "10" and "Outside Flamingo," scribbled in pencil.

The note worried her. She connected it to the dwindling amount of physical contact she experienced with Adam over the past year. Even further back, if she were willing to admit it. They used to make love every weekend, but gradually the frequency changed, and in the past year there had been none at all. In wanting sex, Liz was shy and cautious. From the start she had always looked to Adam to initiate. For Liz the frequency sufficed until, over the past couple of years, it didn't. She felt that, emotionally, Adam had moved offshore, bound who knew where, but in his boat, alone. At times, looking at him unawares, seeing him staring at nothing in particular, she doubted even he knew whither the boat was headed. She couldn't decide if her unsatisfied desire was real or imagined. Had she wanted to understand the signs, she might have thought something was amiss in their relationship some time ago, but she didn't. She tucked the idea away, choosing not to imagine specifics. Maybe, she reasoned, the passion ebbed naturally with an aging marriage, like the tide, but didn't come back the way tides do. She saw but didn't try to think through what she was experiencing to get a better grip on things. She had always been of a mind that viewed jealousy as a weakness. Seeking the truth frightened her enough to close her mind to the changing behavior of the man who shared her bed. So, why didn't she throw away the note? Paper is tangible, fear is a feeling that comes and goes.

She took down from her shelf the book on city restaurants, expecting to find the Flamingo. She then found it in the phone book and dialed the number. A machine said the place was closed until 6pm. She called the number scribbled on the note. A man answered. He sounded half-asleep. Liz asked his name.

"This is Bernic. What's it about, lady?"

Her breathing grew labored and heavy. "Do you know Adam Hudson?"

There was a long pause before Bernie said "Is this some kind of joke?"

"Can you tell me about the Flamingo?" She held her breath waiting for the answer, which was slow to come.

"Not much. But this much: It's not the place for you, Lady." He hung up.

Liz thought about the bathhouses in the West Village. She had read about gay sex in the glory days of the 1970s, when, unaware of the virus, gays in the City came out in all kinds of ways following the Stonewall Riots. But at first she thought Flamingo was a restaurant. But, when she looked up its number, she saw it was in the West Village. Not a place for her, he said. Could Flamingo be one of those bathhouses, she wondered. And, if so, what does it have to do with my Adam?

Responding to a plea from Liz, conveyed to his secretary, Adam arrived at their apartment at 6:30, tired but pleased with a successful day of negotiating, a process he typically entered in fear and emerged with satisfaction. He would get what he wanted, not with guile or muscle but rather from mastery of the facts and the law and their planned and careful application. He wasn't smarter than the guy on the opposite side of the table; just far better prepared. His office skill was as unstoppable as an avalanche. In navigating on the home front, however, he entered with over-confidence, often discovering that the surefooted and fingered skills and instincts on display in the office failed him. His triangular set of relationships with Liz and George had always been a challenge, one that repeatedly surprised him, one he did his best to meet, but never with the firm grasp that seemed to come naturally to him in his practice.

Adam took off his coat, dropped his briefcase and gave Liz the light kiss on the cheek they both were accustomed to.

"Let's talk in the kitchen. I have some things on the stove. Get yourself a drink."

Drink in hand, he came into the kitchen and dropped into his usual chair, from which he could see what Liz was doing and offer his underdeveloped sous-chef skills.

Liz had her long hair neatly tucked into a bun. Over a workaday dress she wore an apron. Facing the stove, she asked what the Flamingo was.

He put down his drink. He felt light-headed, suddenly scared. "Where did that come from? I've never heard of the Flamingo," he snarled in an angry whispering tone.

Liz turned to face him. Her voice a tremble. "Really? You've never been there?"

"No."

"This was in your shirt pocket." Her hand shook as she passed Adam the note.

Adam had been caught in a lie. He had long known it was past time to exit the closet, at least within his own home. Hadn't Liz just opened the door, about to yank him out if he didn't emerge voluntarily? For a year and more he had been tormented, wanting to tell Liz the truth, knowing he had to come clean with his wife. But again and again, shame subdued instinct.

He remembered himself in shorts, in a city park, going behind a tree, raising the pants on his left leg, taking his penis in hand and peeing. He remembered the exquisitely painful shame that showered over him like heavy rain when a policeman emerged from around the tree to face him. The memory vanished as swiftly as it came, leaving him to face his wife. He said "Excuse me a second, I need the john. Be right back."

He moved swiftly to the bathroom, shutting the door behind him. What was he going to tell Liz? The Flamingo, a celebrated disco and bathhouse. He saw the crowd, beautiful male bodies tightly packed, the touching, the wet flesh, all brawn, all shirtless, the mirrored panels clouded over with salt and sweat, the lightshow flashing on and off, the uniformly muscular limbs swaying to the hard beat of music. Many small rooms adjoining the disco. He knew the Flamingo as he knew the palms of his hands. None of this could he explain to his wife. He didn't even see how he could explain Bernie's note, which involved meeting Bernie and a friend of his, outside the Flamingo, a place easy to find. They had no intention of entering the place.

Returning to the kitchen table, he sat down, took his drink in hand, took a long gulp and stared at the stove.

"I'm a gay man, Liz. And I've kept it from you. Appalling, but there it is. Till now I've ducked, imagining the hurt my secret would cause. A weak excuse, but I clung to it. I know, this must be like a scab that's suddenly torn off a wound you didn't even know you had. If there were an excuse, here's what it would be. It's taken years for the reality to sink in. And then some years more before acceptance. At first, whenever the thought appeared, I repressed it. Through college, law school and our marriage. It kept returning. And, I gave way to the urge. At first, I dismissed it as a one-off, an experiment. But it became more frequent, harder to dismiss. Now the fact of my sexuality is clear. And, finally, I realize I need to align that fact with my life, as a whole, instead of leading two separate lives, as I've tried to do for the past couple of years—poorly."

Liz had not wanted to know. She had been like a blind woman beginning to feel an elephant, an animal she had never seen, and suddenly afraid, pulling back, not wanting to learn the full shape and size of it.

"I need time to digest this—I mean, is it revelation, deception, deceit? Or all three? You seem so composed. I'm angry and you're making me angrier with your ridiculous cool. Back off; give me time." Tears rolled down her cheeks, triggering more of the same on Adam's stricken face.

"Wait Liz. Let me go on."

She had turned to go. He reached for her arm, trying, without success, to hold on against her will. "Wait a second. Listen to me. Please. First, what sorrow I feel. I want to apologize. And, if possible, seek some understanding. And make amends. Somehow we've got to come to terms with this. Our lives will go on. And George's. We've got to adjust to the reality. It won't go away. Neither of us can make it go away."

"It's taken you how many years to "adjust to the reality", as you put it? And now you expect me to adjust over one drink? Yeah, let's get real. You lied about the Flamingo." Her voice firm, anger controlled, smoldering.

"Yeah, okay. It's a disco and bathhouse in the West Village. I used to go there. But I gave it up. I've got a partner now. We aren't—neither of us is promiscuous. He has a place in Brooklyn."

"I've heard gays have hundreds, maybe more, sexual encounters in these places, often anonymous. At least, oh, God, at least until AIDS." Liz looked hard at her husband, quizzical, accusing, anger rising again at the thought of the virus.

"Adam, are you part of that disgusting scene?" Suddenly she had realized that, over the past two years, they had had sex, not often and not rewarding, but sex that would have exposed her to AIDS if Adam were infected. "Tell me you weren't."

Adam blanched from a rush of shame, guilt and fear, emotions that tumbled against each other in his brain, almost ripping off the armored pretense of his shallow confidence.

"Look, Liz, whether I was or not is not important. I have Bernie, we are a couple. We know about AIDS. We aren't infected. Of this we are sure. What's past is done with, gone. Not prologue. Trust me," he pleaded.

"I hear you but it doesn't do it for me. Frankly, I'm terrified. Why should I trust you now? After all this. Does the firm know?"

Liz was a keeper of lists. They began in her head, but she was quick to write them down in her ever-present red book. She started down that road now, putting aside the undeveloped feelings she knew would start to evolve later that night, depriving her of sleep. Whether to talk to her doctor? Can one test for HIV? AIDS? How to tell George? Steps to separation. To divorce. Need for a lawyer. Who gets the house? She knew the list was long—longer than the night she would devote to compiling it.

"No!" he replied, voice rising to make it clear how impossible that would be. Two of my partners do; you can guess who. As for trust, does it help to know that Bernie and I trust each other one hundred percent?"

"Trust?" Liz shouted, her face reddening as she glared at him. "I trusted you for how many years? Don't talk to me of trust."

Adam reached across the table for her hand, sorrow embedded across his face.

Liz rose from the table, avoiding contact.

"As I said, I need time on this one. I want to be alone. You can sleep in George's room."

❧ 4 ☙

1978-1981

As best Adam could tell, he was the oldest gay man in the firm, which was among the most prominent in the City. Within the legal profession, there was a grapevine that enabled gays from the elite law schools to learn what firms were likely to be more tolerant than others. Except for two of his partners, who kept their knowledge secret, Adam was not known in the firm to be a homosexual. By choice, he was not listed in the "Princeton Gay Alumni Directory," as it was known, a secret source of information and support. Nor the similar one for Harvard Law. But, judging by the number of calls he got from law students seeking information and advice regarding firms that were the most receptive, or likely to be, Adam seemed to be known in the gay grapevine, and through his success as a partner of Bundy, Rogers & Freund, the firm had developed an image of a place where gays were accepted, whether in the closet, selectively out or fully open to the awareness of others.

Of course, much of that acceptance came about because of Adam's responses to these calls. He was a master at conveying the truth about the firm's ethos and integrity, at least as he saw things, and that truth had a compelling bite to it. Over the years, Adam's message had resulted in the firm attracting a disproportionate number of gays. And the hidden feedback loop led to this imbalance growing. Within the firm, Adam was known to, and knew, all of the incoming gays. And, as the numbers grew, so too did their comfort in being accepted. None of this was in the firm's Operations Manual or mentioned at the partners' weekly lunch.

The partners met in a nearby hotel every Tuesday to review over lunch the firm's business, applaud new clients and tend to the normal range of issues arising in a large multi-city law office of international standing. New undertakings had to be approved by the New Business Committee, and new pro bono matters needed first to be cleared by the Pro Bono Committee. Over many years the firm had developed a prominent reputation for its commitment to work affected with some public interest for which it would not be paid, except through reputational kudos. But this well warranted reputation was more than its own reward. Desirable students were attracted to the firm for this reason. Of course, with the introduction of The American Lawyer, a publication that made a splash by obtaining, and publishing annually, the large firms' net income and profits per partner, students unavoidably began examining the bottom line, and were, far more than before this publication appeared on the scene, attracted by a firm's economic success, the pursuit of which was in constant tension with the question of how much pro bono work to take on.

At one luncheon in 1978, Peter Richardson, the Chair of the Pro Bono Committee, announced the firm had been asked by leaders of the gay community in the City to undertake, pro bono, a test case against New York's Sodomy Law.

Peter informed his partners that the law, on the books for more than a century, and modified periodically, criminalized sodomy even among consenting adults and included both oral and anal sex.

He said that, due to the sensitivity of the matter, his Committee wanted to get the firm's thoughts before proceeding further. He explained that the Committee felt good, indeed, proud to have been picked for this litigation, was unanimous in wanting to accept the assignment, and thought the case would be an easy one to win.

Adam's first reaction, on hearing Peter's remarks, was to think he must leave the meeting, that it was the right thing to do since the discussion would obviously raise for him a conflict of interest.

But only two partners knew Adam's sexual identity, and to exit the meeting would be to exit the closet. He stayed put.

The firm's reputation was applauded by some, who opined that, of course, they must take the matter on, both to confirm that reputation and extend it. Others worried about the effect that the case could have on their fee-paying business clients. Concern for the firm's major (in terms of fees) Japanese client, the Mitsubishi group, was circled as an especially delicate matter.

Robert Russell, the partner principally in charge of this client, predicted it would drop the firm. "Japanese have no taste for homosexuals," Robert said.

One partner claimed that, by becoming involved, they would turn highly desirable students and Supreme Court clerks away. Adam felt desperate to respond. He would argue that being identified with the case as counsel for the plaintiffs would attract more students and clerks than it turned away. But he kept quiet, hoping that someone else would advance this point. In fact, within minutes, as if he had read his friend's thought, Roger Scragg made this claim.

Partners began repeating themselves. George Banville, the Chairman, a euphemism for operations head of firm, brought the matter to an end by declaring that his "sense of the firm" was not to take the case on.

Adam knew that "sense" was more one man's view than a consensus. He felt wounded, particularly by George Banville, for whom he had done more work than for any other senior during his years as an associate. A leader who, since arriving at the firm, Adam had admired, particularly for the personal values he now realized had existed chiefly in his imagination. Glancing around the room, Adam caught the eyes of Charlie and Roger, who, he could see from their pained expressions, were feeling vicariously Adam's suffering.

Gay lawyers in the City were astonished by the firm's decision. Its reputation as a leader in the pro bono field took a hit. The excuse that 'clients would object' was close to incomprehensible. A full explanation would require a measurement of the degree of homophobia in the firm, something impossible to even contemplate. Adam knew that should he ask George Banville if there was any homophobia among the partners, he would answer "zero." "Contrary to our ethos," he would declare, demanding to know how one could even imagine such a thing.

In twos or threes, perhaps, over lunch or an after-hours drink, the firm's decision was rehearsed and dissected. Adam was confronted by some of the more aggressive gay associates, seeking some reason for the apparent gulf between the firm's pretense and its practice. To most, the best explanation seemed to be a generational divide—an embedded homophobia in the older group of partners, who, on a matter of such delicacy, felt entitled to decide regardless of majority view—a view deliberately and with skill left unexplored.

In 1980, in NY v. Onofre, the New York Court of Appeals ruled the sodomy law unconstitutional. Adam rejoiced over the result, while still suffering the assaults on his way of life that occurred at that unfortunate firm lunch. As Peter Richardson reported at a lunch soon after the decision was handed down, "The firm passed up a great opportunity for an easy win. It was Reese, Mueller who took the case after we declined the honor, and they carried it to victory. Tant pis."

Adam's take on Onofre was not so much the glory missed by his firm but its failure to stand by some important values it often publicly claimed to possess, ones that seemed to him to have been ignored in the partner debate, ones, in fact, he had used to woo gay law students. My God, Adam thought, even the New York City Bar Association took a position on the matter, filing an amicus brief in support of repeal. He believed his silence contributed to the firm's embarrassing position. He felt implicated, guilty. His failure on top of failure by his firm.

5

1982

Can a gay tell if another man is gay? How long does it take to tell? What are the clues? Adam often wondered. As far as the firm's partners went, all were straight and he had no concern that his particular life style was known or even suspected by the others. And, yet, when a new hire arrived, if he were gay, Adam could tell in the space of minutes. He had no litmus test, only the use of his five senses. In combination, they would swiftly detect any gay lawyer who crossed the firm's threshold, as easily as a mosquito detects blood. Adam's insight regarding gays was hardly unique with him. Most gays had the same ability. It was a brotherhood, easy to identify if you were a brother, akin to a special handshake identifying members of a final club at Harvard. This meant that incoming gays ignorant of Adam's sexuality would typically pick up his scent as quickly as he did theirs.

Adam had a strict set of rules designed to protect reputations and jobs, not least his own, but others as well. They boiled down to three: never indulge with anyone at the firm, anyone from a client of the firm, or anyone in a relationship with a friend. The rules kept him out of trouble, but occasionally not without a struggle or some devious ingenuity.

The firm represented Turner, one of the City's large private foundations. Almost all of the firm's partners, as a matter of firm ethos, were assiduous in not referring to a client as "mine," even though the partner might be the one in charge or have been the one attracting the client to the firm. The concept was centripetal, designed to strengthen the idea of a cohesive firm, to which all partners owed loyalty. In theory, no client was owned by one partner; all were clients of the firm. The partners recognized that the theory, in certain cases, didn't hold water, in the sense that certain clients came to the firm because of a single partner's connection and would follow that partner elsewhere, were the partner to leave. Like many firm values, the pretense wasn't supported by the reality at all times and in all cases. But for the vast majority of clients, yes. And, because the firm was highly successful from many angles, with remarkably few exceptions, partners didn't leave for supposedly greener pastures.

Adam was in charge of Turner and, with a team of three associates, handled both the financial and grant-making sides of this prominent institution. He worked mainly with Reginald Smith, the Financial Vice President, who had come to Turner following a similar job at a Midwestern university and an unsuccessful fling with politics in seeking election to the House of Representatives.

Reginald was a polymath and to no degree shy about displaying it—first as proof, then as dazzle. This Adam recognized after their first lunch together in Turner's lunch room. The urgency with which Reginald dashed across the menu of his chosen topics, in scope far broader than the lunch room's offerings, suggested to Adam a boy just past puberty who was sharing a beer with his first date and, with an excessive amount of pent-up energy, was determined to prove his intellectual worth. Failure, Adam sensed, was not a common experience for Reginald, but one he probably handled well, as evidenced by his very brief political career.

At that lunch, Reginald brought along a young man about half his age, introducing him as Malcolm Flynn, an economist who would be working with Reginald in managing Turner's large endowment. Malcolm was blond, handsome in a youthful way and physically fit. He was a contrast to Reginald, who looked older than his 60 years and had a mop of curly white hair sprinkled with black remnants of younger days atop a lean distinguished face that might best be described as Senatorial.

When Reginald excused himself for a few minutes during lunch, Malcolm astonished Adam by declaring in hushed voice that he was no economist. In fact, he'd never even taken a course in the subject. He suggested it was just Reginald's little exaggeration, one he had objected to more than once but gotten nowhere with his boss. Adam pondered just what role Malcolm Flynn would fill. He felt his antenna picking up signs of homosexuality.

That afternoon he got a call from Reginald's wife, Louise, a woman he'd never met or spoken to. Introducing herself, she spoke in nervous whispers. She claimed Reginald had brought Malcolm to Turner to continue their relationship. They were lovers. Reginald was bisexual, Louise said, but perhaps more inclined toward males than females. She begged Adam to help send Malcolm away. "Please," she said, "find some way, any way you want, to get rid of him."

Adam was dumbfounded. Perhaps, her voice coming weakly over the phone, he had misheard. She repeated the request. Adam told Louise that he was not really in a position, as Turner's outside lawyer, to do what she asked of him. "I've only today met your husband. And Mr. Flynn. What you ask is an exceedingly delicate matter for anyone," Adam said. "But for one in my position, it raises a dilemma. A serious conflict of interest. As you can see, Mrs. Smith, I barely know either of them. I represent Turner. And this is not a legal matter for Turner. Please understand, I'm not the right man to help you." With that, Louise let Adam off the hook, deep resignation sounding through the phone.

I mean, what could I do, Adam asked himself after putting down the phone, still shocked by the request. "Weird," he thought, that was one word for it. He would have thought it unbelievable if he had not just heard her tell the same story twice.

Adam found working with Reginald often stressful, always demanding, always a challenge. And, to a degree, even enjoyable, when the day's work was over, like the feeling one has after finishing a strenuous run on an inclined treadmill. Beyond his intelligence, he was energetic, imaginative and reckless, a combination designed to tax a lawyer's skills, ranging from the law to human relations. He made Adam feel not only useful but needed, even at times essential, which for a lawyer made him the perfect client.

What Adam was disappointed about, following Louise's call, was his failure to have identified either Reginald or Malcolm as one of his tribe. He just hadn't paid much attention to the signs he saw in Malcolm, dismissing them as improbable. But missing Reginald surprised him. Perhaps it was due to Reginald's broader sexual palette, although Adam's was seemingly as broad. He couldn't explain the lapse, which seemed especially strange, given his lunch with the two lovers. What he also missed was Louise's suffering. His focus was on the client, and those representing it. He wondered how much Turner's President knew when he hired Reginald, or if anyone at the foundation was aware. To a certainty, he believed that Turner's General Counsel, the soul of naïveté, was not.

Reginald decided to increase the endowment's allocation to real estate from a measly 2% to a range of 12-15%, and, like everything else he decided to do, to execute fast. Commitments flew out of the office with uncommon, and often unwise, speed. One early commitment was for a large investment in rental apartments in Denver. It soon necessitated a trip to Denver to negotiate final terms. Reginald planned the trip, giving Adam the dates and saying he would book travel and hotel accommodations. "Have you ever stayed at the Brown Palace? You're going to love it. An 1892 landmark. See you at the airport. We can develop strategy and key terms on the plane."

At the airport, Reginald gave Adam an uncommonly tight hug, accompanied by what Adam took to be a soft pelvic thrust. He couldn't dismiss these signals, which, coming on top of Louise's telephone call, were in the nature of red flags. When they arrived at the hotel, Adam discovered Reginald had booked only one room, and that with only one bed, a king-size. Given the routine customs of business trips, Reginald's booking was unheard of—bizarre. Adam was afraid he might put the client relationship in jeopardy if he demanded a separate room. But, he knew he couldn't sleep in the same bed with Reginald. He saw no escape from needing a separate room. He would have to risk losing the client to secure it.

Adam decided to address the matter at the reception desk, and to do so by simply asking the clerk for another room, mentioning that the booking had been intended. He avoided looking at Reginald while speaking to the clerk. The gambit worked, at least for the moment. A second room was booked, a key provided and Adam's bags assigned to his room. Adam had to imagine Reginald's disappointment, even anger, because his client showed no emotion, and uttered not a word, as the transaction was completed and they rode up in the elevator together.

That night, they both felt the exuberance and freedom that comes with an escape from one's office to a top-flight hotel in some interesting city. They ordered martinis straight up with a twist before dinner and picked an intense Brunello di Montalcino to share with the meal. They both ordered artichokes vinaigrette with lamb chops to follow.

Looking at their respective plates after the artichokes had been consumed, Reginald found amusement, if not wonder, at the difference in design. The spent leaves on his plate were strewn haphazardly here and there, the result of impatient tosses. In contrast, Reginald noted on Adam's plate a battalion of leaves, each following the one in front with exquisite precision around the perimeter of the plate to form a perfect circle.

"Adam, it's about your plate. How do you explain such care in marshalling those spent leaves? I've never seen anything like it. Look at mine."

"Yes, it's the way I do it. Why is a fair question. Early toilet training? Who knows? In my home, discipline ruled in all things growing up. I'm afraid this may be one result."

Adam kept to himself the metaphor he saw on his client's plate, leaves stripped quickly and tossed here and there, like the real estate deals Reginald was signing with reckless speed.

They decided to pass on dessert. Espresso followed as they tidied up some loose ends for the negotiation that would take place the next morning. Much to Adam's relief, no mention had been made of the single room incident. Perhaps the booking was a mistake. He felt in the clear with client bruises, if any, not serious, well on their way to healing.

Leaning over the table within six inches of Adam's face, Reginald said, *sotto voce*, "About the room—in that king size bed I had imagined we would have some sport. I don't get it, because I always know. At least I thought I did. Where did I go wrong?"

Reginald's candor hit him hard, like an unexpected punch in the solar plexus. He should have seen it coming, given the hotel booking. He resented being so easily identified. It mortified him. Later, tossing around in bed, he knew what's sauce for the goose is sauce for the gander: his ability to detect gays was nothing special. Other gays possessed the same skill, as Reginald had proved over dinner.

Recovering, Adam decided to meet his client's candor with some of his own. It seemed the right thing to do. And, beyond that, it could turn the room incident from a threat into an exercise in bonding.

"Reg, your reading was dead-on. My resistance to the single room is the result of some personal rules. So, there you have it. Nothing more nor less than a cobbler sticking to his last. Your record for insight is secure."

They left the table and hugged, with Reginald applying the now familiar thrust; then before Reginald could turn away, Adam held his arm and said: "As a child did your parents hug you a lot?"

"Why, yes, of course they did, and often, through good times and bad. Why do you ask?"

Mumbling something about curiosity, Adam said, "Time for bed." They journeyed to their separate rooms for the night. Thinking about his client's signature embrace, Adam imagined he must use it as an inviting exploration with selected friends, as commonplace to them as extending one's hand to a stranger.

6

1954-1959

As an only child, Adam received more attention than a kid in a large family. The attention could be described as carrot and stick, with Hannah wielding the carrot and Wright the stick. Obedience and discipline were foremost in the minds of his parents. He was spanked often, for offenses large and small, the vigor of the exercise depending on how serious, in Wright's opinion, the cause. Corporal punishment ended at the threshold of high school in Mamaroneck. Adam had no recall of these spankings, except for the ones caused by stealing and by mishandling the family cat, each remarkably painful.

He applied to Princeton, his first choice, and was accepted. He imagined how delighted his parents would be at the news. At dinner that night, Wright congratulated Adam and then questioned him about how his close school friends had done.

"Father, each was accepted by his first choice. Yale, Dartmouth, MIT and Penn. Great news, don't you think? And a blue ribbon for the school, for public education."

Wright got that peculiar expression on his face that signaled an idea had popped into his head. When this 'light bulb' turned on, he would keep the idea under cover until he had the attention of the entire room. He could be patient. In his law classes at Columbia, he never had to wait long. At home he squinted, brushed one side of his nose with an index finger, then stroked his chin once or twice before speaking. Having been through the drill innumerable times, both wife and son knew they were about to hear something Wright considered important, even profound.

"You were especially fortunate, Adam, to have in your class several competitors of outstanding scholarly ability. As an incoming tide lifts all boats, I think you were carried forward, let's say energized, by these classmates. You owe them some thanks. Indeed, we all do."

Hannah saw how crestfallen Adam was. In intellectual capacity, she considered herself inferior to her husband. And she knew, to a certainty, that Wright thought so too, and treated her accordingly. In truth, she didn't consider herself an intellectual at all. Over the years, Wright's dismissal of her created a feedback loop, causing her to express to Wright her thoughts, and in time her feelings too, with less and less frequency. Perhaps this could explain Hannah's features, which over years of marriage became creased with care and worry. But this was her son.

Hannah stood up. "I'll get the salad. But, let me say something." Turning to look at Adam, her voice rising, she said, "Getting into Princeton is a great achievement—one that was yours alone."

"Thank you, Mother. A generous thought. But Father has a point. It's like drafting in a bicycle race."

"Yes, no harm in drafting. Son, it's a great chance. Some impressive names connected to Princeton. Einstein for one. Wilson for another. The challenge is to squeeze out all that the college offers. You've got the potential. Initiate. Go beyond the assignments. Get to know your professors. You've heard me on this before. It's just a matter of applying yourself—nose to the grindstone, as we used to say in Montana. For college is a competition. Here's another western saying, one I'd forgotten: 'He who builds the fire gets warm first.'"

By the time he arrived on the Princeton campus, Adam believed he had homosexual leanings. The idea terrified him. The thought of how Wright would react to his feelings was enough, alone, to dissuade him from exploring his sexuality. Recalling an incident in school when he was a thirteen-year-old on the verge of entering puberty, he tried out the notion that it had been a dream. Could it have happened just in his head?

It was a gorgeous afternoon in April. He and one of his good friends, Roger Roebling, were stretched out on their backs on the abundant green turf of an athletic field not in use.

They were less than an inch apart. Roger developed an erection.

Adam had one too. He moved his hand, slowly, cautiously, reaching over to feel under his pants for Roger's cock.

Without talking, even in a whisper, they seemed to be guided by similar feelings. They rolled over, unbuttoned their pants and began to explore the other's sex in detail. In time they began kissing each other while continuing the play. Into the mix they introduced tongues. Adam felt consumed with arousal. It was new and exciting, beyond his previous experience or imagination. The ringing of a school bell brought this virginal episode to an end. Buttoning up, awkward and guilty, as if the bell had been a spy recording their every move, or God's signal for expulsion from their little Edenic space, they rose from the grass and returned to the school building, saying not a word to each other.

Adam wished for an encore, but neither he nor Roger was bold enough to suggest such a thing before summer vacation began. By fall, when they returned to school, both had moved well into puberty, with pubic hair fresh and curly like early lettuce, dropped balls as tender as grapes and, for proof, the pleasure of using a hand to make one's cock rock hard with super-charged blood until it erupted with cum, igniting a sharp gasp, followed by *la petite mort* designed by some divinity for males only. Here was a pastime each of them began to enjoy with some frequency. It didn't take them long, upon resuming their classes, to pick up the explorations begun the preceding spring. They found a forest glen within sight of school. There they jerked each other off, sharing these newly discovered joys of puberty. Often they competed by attempting to measure, however imprecisely, the distance achieved at climax by sperm propelled upward. Adam compared it to grapeshot from a cannon.

One afternoon, with sun beams piercing the forest through green leaves that rustled gently in an afternoon breeze, after their practiced orgasms, Roger cautiously asked Adam if he ever considered himself a homosexual.

"I've thought about it. It scares me. But I like girls. I plan on dating. On marriage. A family. I'm just not a homo. How 'bout you?"

Roger stood up. "Not something I think about. No worries."

The boys' outdoor practice was in danger of becoming a habit. It started to interfere with various activities. Roger played soccer and was very committed to it. And gifted. The soccer coach had particular ideas about masturbation. He thought the practice hurtful to training and performance on the field. He told his squad, if they were inclined to indulge, to stop until the season was over or get off the team.

"And this means not just your hands off but those of your friends." His order was emphatic. And he hinted he had ways of discovering infractions.

The coach's directive scared the bejesus out of Roger. He told Adam their trysts were over. Ambition to excel in soccer trumped pleasures of the glen.

From the perspective of a Freshman at Princeton, flush with the zeal to make new friends and aware that openness at the point of entry was important both to appeal to others and invite reciprocity, Adam knew he first had to be true to himself. In recalling his experiments with Roger Roebling, he knew it was no dream. The feelings he had with Roger lurked in the dark corners of his mind, never going away, peeking out on occasion.

The problem was what did being true to himself mean? For the academic side, of course, it meant study and fulfillment, which translated, for his father, into high grades, and for himself, pleasure in the whole process of learning, the accretion of knowledge. But as for his sexuality, there he felt blinded by uncertainty. He dated girls. He was good with girls. They liked him. They let him play around, up to a point. Although he might try to push beyond the point, if resisted, he always backed off. He would occasionally come in his pants from drawn-out petting.

Adam had been a swimmer in high school. A good one, particularly in the crawl. At Princeton, he made the Freshman team. He enjoyed the training and the competition. Swimming, like everything he set out to do, involved seeking his father's advice and approval. Wright used these occasions to drive home his two oft-repeated lessons: "Son, first, don't ever undertake something you aren't prepared to hurl yourself into with total commitment and energy. That's what my father insisted for me. It's what I did. It worked. And, now, it's what I insist for you. And second, don't ever do anything that, if printed in the New York Times, would embarrass me. Or, naturally, your mother."

Although Adam worked hard to perfect the crawl, and was the second best among the freshman swimmers, he never won a race. Wright had been a collegiate swimmer and won a number of races in the butterfly. Through the season, he attended a few of his son's meets, always coming away feeling disappointed in Adam's performance. One evening, when Adam had come home to his parents' house in Mamaroneck after the swimming season was over, Wright asked his son how many races he had won.

"None, Father."

"And how many seconds and thirds?"

"No seconds. Two thirds."

Adam watched his father rub his index finger up and down the side of his nose.

"That's surprising, given your genes—you know—your potential. Over the season, I suppose you didn't try as hard as you could have."

"That's not it, Father. I busted my butt training. If anything, I overdid it. There were zero distractions. I believe I was as fast as my potential allowed."

Wright shook his head slowly, narrowed his eyes and muttered, "If you say so ..."

Despite not being a star, Adam was popular with his teammates and they with him. After a training session, or a meet, the team typically showered together. Although he strived to fight back the tide that swirled in his head upon entering the open showers, he couldn't avoid admiring the smooth muscular limbs, tight buttocks and washboard stomachs of his fellow swimmers, reminding him of Michelangelo's statue of David in the Accademia Gallery in Florence. That sculpture was a favorite of Wright's, who had made a study of it in college and seemed sometimes obsessed by Michelangelo's ability to bring to life a block of marble.

Soaking in the shower's heat, Adam marveled at the cocks, large and small, straight and bent, light and dark, emerging from forests of pubic hair, thick and thin, wheat-blond and raven-black. Avert his eyes? Impossible. He was drawn particularly to Henry Wolfson, who came from Hartford, Connecticut, and swam the butterfly. Adam thought the attraction went both ways. Adam told himself it was just a growing friendship, but he felt something more, something centered in the groin. The shower scenes hammered Adam with a jumble of feelings, at once delightful and frightening.

On one training day, it happened that Henry and Adam were left in the pool alone, doing laps in their respective specialties. Someone, not noticing their presence, turned off the lights, leaving only early evening brightness through the windows, enough to see around the room. Whether by accident or not, Henry and Adam collided in the pool and moved together, touching here and there as they went to the shallow end. There they embraced, each having grown erect on the short journey. Feeling Henry's cock, Adam kissed Henry, his tongue thrusting between open lips. They pulled down their suits and Henry turned Adam around 180 degrees and thrust his cock in the orifice on offer. After Henry came, Adam reciprocated. They left the pool, Adam recalling Masaccio's fresco of Adam and Eve's *Expulsion from the Garden of Eden*. He felt shame too, compounded by the memory of his first time with Roger Roebling. He averted Henry's eyes.

In the showers, Adam tried to avoid looking at Henry, and when he did, looked only from the waist up.

Adam said: "I don't know what came over me in the pool. I've never done this before. Perhaps you have. For me, never again."

"Never? Why not?"

"I plan on marriage, a family." His voice rising, he said "I'm not a homosexual."

Henry looked at Adam, trying to catch his eye, a quizzical expression shaping his face.

"I hear you," he said in a tone dripping with doubt.

Adam pondered the pool incident almost to death. He wrung its neck as if it were a chicken bound for the oven. Helplessly, he sought certainty about his sexual identity. Did he tilt toward homosexuality by dint of genes? The same gene set his father claimed should make him a star in the pool. He dared to imagine what his father would think of the sort of co-starring role he assumed with Henry? Funny, and yet not so funny. Nothing in his upbringing or schooling seemed to explain his ambiguous condition. Deep uncertainty. Fear and, at times, self-alienation.

From Adam's early childhood, Wright Alexander Hudson had insisted on knowing his son's mind. He imagined that by discovering his son's thoughts, he could shape them, and through them, his behavior. He viewed this effort as the compelling obligation of a parent. Wright's desire for this relationship became urgent when, a couple of years after Adam's birth, Hannah was informed by her gynecologist that she'd be unable to have more children.

Wright's sense of parental duty to shape Adam led him, one evening, sitting with Hannah in their kitchen over a nightcap, to what he called 'an inspiration.' Seeing Wright's index finger, rubbing his nose, Hannah knew before she heard.

"In sculpting David, Michelangelo had to remove the excess marble. In contrast, we mold a baby, not by removal, but by adding over time. Not just weight. Intelligence, experience. Maybe even wisdom. Do you find this as exciting an insight as I do?"

"Interesting, yes. Exciting, not much. My goodness, it's getting late. I'm for bed. Do you want to finish your drink?"

One outcome of Wright's parental theory was Adam's willingness to share his thoughts and seek the advice of his father. He could have gone the other way, clamming up or even lying. But Adam responded exactly as his father had planned. Like a dog trained to fetch and return a ball, Adam brought Wright his successes and his failures, his ambitions and his fears, his hopes and even his dreams. Unlike a dog, he did so without the treats that the trainer typically doles out. But there remained a few subjects that, even with his particular upbringing, his willing response to his father's demands, and his simple instinct for openness, Adam kept to himself. His playtime with Roger Roebling, and his experience with Henry Wolfson, were two examples.

Another was masturbation. It was a subject, Adam believed, his father could help him come to terms with. But the thought of taking his questions to Dwight was very uncomfortable, and grew more so as he sketched the way the talk might go. It cast his mind into turmoil.

Wright pre-empted his son, having observed the beginnings of pubic hair when Adam exited the shower. It took him back to his own puberty, his confusion with its meaning and, growing up isolated on a Montana farm, his need for parental help, which he neither asked for nor received. Indeed, before puberty, his father had abused him until one day his mother saw her husband in the act of forcing himself on their son. Her scream was something Wright could never forget. It must have erected a shield, for Wright's father never again came to him bent on abuse. For Wright, what his father did to him was kept secret, revealed to no one, not even Hannah. In his mind it was a deep stain on his life, one he shared with his father, despite having never given consent.

With puberty, Wright felt acutely the need to masturbate. It seemed to consume him, while at the same time scaring him. He felt guilt in the doing, failure in not being able to stop, and isolation in having no one to consult. The pain of that experience had lasted in his mind. He resolved with Adam to address the subject, confident he would be fulfilling a fatherly duty, confident he knew how best to do it.

In the methodical way of a law professor who took everything seriously, especially himself, especially how he spent his time (the wasting of which he considered criminal), he informed Adam they were going to have a "birds and bees" talk. He assigned a time—Saturday at nine—and a place—Wright's home office—for the purpose.

That office felt like the inner sanctum of a cathedral. Early morning sunlight beamed through the only window, a large casement opposite an imposing, impeccably neat desk behind which, Adam imagined, Wright would sit for hours, body ramrod stiff, mind sharp and focused, thinking hard, grappling with intellectually challenging issues of contract law, much as a priest might grapple with the paradoxes of Christianity.

The door to Wright's office was always closed. No one, not even Hannah, was permitted entry without first knocking and being invited in. Anticipating the "birds and bees" visit to his father's private space, Adam had the preposterous thought that his father might use the office to masturbate. After all, he and Hannah, at his insistence, had separate bedrooms, a change occurring when Adam was twelve. Might they have separate outlets for sexual urges? In the privacy of his mind, Adam often entertained bizarre thoughts, driven by a pleasure he found in keeping them secret. He couldn't avoid it. And he was sure other boys his age had similar fantasies. His friend, Roger Roebling, had admitted to it.

Adam's thought of his father drifted to ways and means. How, given the lack of a sink or shower, would Father manage? Cum-stiff trousers? Tissues in the waste basket? Possible clues to look for. From some distant place, from a separate brain, Adam looked down at these thoughts and marveled at how bizarre, how absurd they were. They must remain his alone.

Like down-east coastal fog subdued by the first rays of a bright penetrating sun, this line of thought vanished when Adam knocked on his father's door. It was precisely nine.

Wright welcomed his son, indicating the chair he should sit in.

"You know our topic, this morning: Birds and Bees."

Wright launched into a recital of how men and women, upon marriage, engage with each other to have offspring. He was well into the science of the subject when an insight brought him to a dead stop.

"Is this biology a matter you are familiar with? If so, and I see from your nod and your expression, that it is, we should move on to the more difficult issues—not ones of how but of whether and when for a Christian life, a moral life, the one I know you want to pursue."

"Father, let me ask you a question. It relates to religion. I have attended church all these years, been baptized and gone through confirmation into the faith, gone to church on Sundays, sung in the choir, even been paid ten cents a rehearsal—in all a big commitment to Christianity, and yet I've never caught a word about the role of sex. Why?"

Finger to nose, Wright narrowed his eyes in what Adam knew was his father's way of implying deep thought, but now more than that, an expression of appreciation for the question he was pondering.

"I've never thought about that. I think you're right. The Church must think matters of sex are best left in the clerical closet. Hey! Neat alliteration, don't you think?"

"Perhaps the thought being that the parents of every child will discuss the subject in ways best designed for that family. Of course, as you probably know from bull-sessions, very few parents actually have that talk, the one we are just now starting. I think, for most families, sex education remains closeted by parents and the Church. This leaves the subject open to false and misleading gossip, even fantasies, among kids."

"Father, you nailed it. Most parents must not see it that way."

"Yes, but calling it a duty doesn't make it any easier. With my parents, and growing up, it's all a blank. Now, I want to speak of having sex and masturbation. The moral code is really quite simple. Sex with a woman only if you are married to her. And never masturbate. A very slippery slope. Both axioms flow from the Bible. And beyond that both are sound rules for a moral life, whatever religion you might pursue. Sex can become an addiction, just as bad, or worse, than opium. Pursued outside these rules, one can experience mental, physical and spiritual problems. They can harm your life. So, do you understand? Will you agree to abide by this code?"

"Yes, Father, I promise to try. You say the Bible condemns masturbation?"

"Yes, it's immoral. That's right out of the Bible. Here, hand me the good book. I'll read you one passage."

As Adam took down the Bible from his father's bookshelf, he itched to ask Wright if he had ever masturbated. But doing so was too scary, too much like a challenge, an invasion of his father's privacy. In silence, he handed over the book.

Wright flipped to a page he had visited before. He announced the passage was from Corinthians 6:18 and began to read in solemn tone, like a Priest enlightening his flock:

"Every other sin that man commits is outside the body, but the immoral man sins against his own body."

"So, Adam, there you have it."

"I suppose you can read it that way."

""Adam, that's the only way to read the passage. Scholars read it that way and they know. But if you're still not convinced, I can give you another Biblical injunction. Genesis, Chapter 38. Oman was put to death by God because he 'wasted his seed on the ground,' as the good book puts it, instead of seeding his brother's wife, as directed by Judah, his father.

Adam felt subdued by his father's command of the Bible. "Okay, I'm convinced. But, just to cover all the bases, what about homosexuals? Where do they fit in?"

"Homosexuality? It's a pathology, a disease, a mental disorder. There is no such thing as a "normal" homosexual. An oxymoron, that's what it is, to be sure. Ha! Adam, I'm sure you know that word. A particularly pungent one, don't you think?"

"Today, psychiatrists consider homosexuality a disease that, with therapy, can be treated, the patient cured. But none of this is something you need concern yourself with. You'll be sticking to girls, hugging and kissing them until you find the right one to marry. And only after the ceremony will you enjoy intercourse—with your wife. It's that simple."

Adam got up to leave Wright's office. Changing his mind, he sat down again across the desk from his father.

"Before I go, may I ask you something?"

"Why of course, son. Shoot."

"It's about your knowledge of the Bible. Your interest in it. And reliance. How did all this happen?"

Wright was not one who could speak easily about his life in Montana, growing up. Just opening that door would cause his face to tighten and his eyes to become intense and focused sharply on the cause of that door being opened.

"My parents considered themselves Christians, but they never attended church. Nor did I. But I started reading the Bible at the suggestion of a teacher when I was twelve. Then I took an elective in the Good Book. My interest in its teachings grew with that course. In time, I mastered it."

"Did your parents encourage you?"

Wright showed discomfort. His right index finger began to rub his nose. For what seemed to Adam minutes of silence, Wright didn't speak.

"Look Adam, I think you should know I was not close to my parents, growing up. I never felt they had my best interests in the things they did with me. I often felt abandoned, alone. Growing up was exceedingly difficult for me. I resolved, in my teens, that if I ever married and had children, I would provide loving guidance from the beginning, and be a role model for them. More than that,

I would do my best to mold them, as the Bible molds those who seek its guidance."

"Father, I really appreciate this background. I can now see how different my upbringing has been from yours."

"Let's keep this story between just us."

7

1952-1955

One of Adam's favorites in 10th grade was Jennifer Stultz, a tall, handsome girl with brown hair streaked with tones of red, a ski-jump nose and naturally peach-toned complexion carried on a figure made to concentrate the minds of her male classmates, a proven distraction from classroom subjects, and an outgoing personality given to banter and fun. He saw her as the yin to his yang, someone appearing, at least, to harbor no hang-ups that might restrain a simple love of life in all its youthful glory. And that was his attraction to her, beyond her athletic skills in field hockey and track, which impressed coaches and classmates alike. If given to boasting, she could have claimed a quirky sense of humor, a gluey retention of jokes and a love for the absurd, but she had no pretense to being an intellectual. Despite efforts to excel in class, her grades were solidly mediocre. She was okay with that. And so were her parents, whose unqualified affection from birth bore no connection to educational achievements.

Adam's reputation among his male classmates was easy, open and welcoming. He was given to jokes and especially limericks, which he tucked away in his brain, as a squirrel hid nuts for the coming winter. He was popular, clearly a leader among the boys. With the girls, however, he was uncertain and shy. Although they had been friends for a couple of years, it took him until the fall of senior year to invite Jennifer out for a date.

Wright and Hannah took intense interest in Adam's choice in girls. The high school was in Mamaroneck and, as Wright put it to Adam when he was entering the first year of high school:

"Your school has the usual mix of students from both the working classes on one side of the Post Road and the professional class on the other. There will be quite a broad spectrum of minorities, as well as a goodly number of students from well-to-do families like ours."

Adam knew there was some fatherly signaling buried beneath his icy analysis but couldn't excavate it and didn't want to expose himself by seeking help.

Jennifer was Adam's first formal date. He took her to see *Lost Horizon,* a classic by Frank Capra, starring Ronald Colman. They met at the theatre. He paid for the tickets from his allowance. Adam offered to walk Jennifer home, but she declined, striking out on her own.

Upon returning from the film, he was faced with a barrage of questions about her from his parents, most of which he couldn't answer. He didn't know her address, didn't know what her parents did, siblings, if any, and other questions he couldn't answer. But they knew from their son's behavior that Jennifer was the first girl in whom he had shown real interest. In that they rejoiced, for he had long shown little interest in the opposite sex.

Wright was dissatisfied with his son's meagre response to questions he considered essential for a responsible parent to know. At his urging, Hannah suggested Adam invite Jennifer for dinner, an idea he did not resist. In fact, he was delighted. They picked a Friday. Hannah asked Adam whether Jennifer was religious. He didn't know but, given the community she lived in, he assumed she came from a Catholic family. Hannah bought halibut. She had the idea of oven-cooking the fish at high temperature, smothered in red peppers, onions and capers. Roasted new potatoes, green salad and, for dessert, various ice creams. She ran the menu by Adam, who expressed surprise.

"I don't recall being invited into your dinner decisions before, mother. Let's keep this thing simple."

"You know, this is the first girl you've ever brought across our doorstep. That's worthy of special attention, and whether you like it or not, you will always remember the occasion, just as you will remember the first girl you kiss. Or should I put that in the past tense?"

She looked hard at him. He wore a smile not easy for her to decipher: Cheshire cat or one who swallowed the canary? Turning on his heels, Adam returned to his room and the day's homework.

At breakfast on the appointed day for Jennifer's visit to the Hudson home, confusion reigned. Adam said he would bring Jennifer home with him, directly from school. Hannah thought this a bad idea, since it would put her in the house at least two hours before even an early dinner, a time when Hannah would be busy trying to pull the meal together.

"She has a bike. Suppose I suggest she ride over around six."

Hannah started to nod approval when Wright raised his hand to arrest her. "That's not the way we Hudsons do things. Bike here? Tasteless. You're growing up a gentleman. A gentleman would escort her to our home. So should you. Do you know her address? Our side of the Post Road or the other?"

"I think she lives on the other side. I'll find out the address and do as you say."

Hannah smiled softly. "Wright, you were well named, my love. You've always been a stickler for style. So, what's the dress code?"

"For Adam, coat and tie. Nothing fancy. For Jennifer, we will see. And learn."

Adam left for school fearing that his father viewed the dinner as the occasion for Jennifer to audition for some ill-defined relationship with his son. Whether as girl friend or just as friend, Adam saw his father assuming the role of grand inquisitor, duty-bound to adduce enough evidence of worthiness to decide, for his son, Jennifer's fate. The process felt all wrong to Adam, and yet he knew Father considered himself, and in fact seemed to Adam to be, seldom, if ever, wrong in his opinions.

Between classes, Adam discussed with Jennifer his plan for the evening. Since their houses were within walking distance of each other, Adam would walk to Jennifer's house, arriving about five, and accompany Jennifer back to the Hudson home. Round-trip, about 45 minutes.

"Adam, that's a nutty plan. I planned on walking over to your house, arriving about six. No need to escort me, silly."

"You're right, of course. The plan wasn't mine. It's Father's plan, and he insists. Says my letting you come on your own would be tasteless. Non-Hudsonian. I'm afraid I'm stuck."

"I see. Your family's honor. Okay. Come around 5:30."

❧

The walk from Jennifer's home to Adam's involved crossing the busy Boston Post Road, which originated in revolutionary times as a system of mail delivery routes between New York City and Boston and evolved into one of the first major highways in the country. Adam guided them to a safe crossing marked by one of the remaining 18th century milestones measuring distances along the road.

"There are few of these left," Adam said.

"What happened to them?" Jennifer asked.

"Who knows? Probably stolen. They were obviously made to last."

"Thieves devoted to history, no doubt!" Aware of how much it pleased him, Jennifer flashed a smile in that certain mischievous way that wrinkled her nose.

"Ah, no doubt," said Adam, meeting her smile with an appreciating one of his own.

The 20-minute walk took them across the Post Road from an area dense with modest houses, well maintained and sited close to streets bare of trees or sidewalks, to a leafy Eden-like area with wider streets, well-kept sidewalks and large, imposing houses set well back from the streets and fronted by carefully groomed lawns of tennis court size or more.

As watchful of Adam's return as she was of the halibut roasting in a hot oven, Hannah was at the door when it opened to admit the couple. Adam introduced Jennifer to his mother from the doorstep, imagining Hannah a worried hen peering into the dark to check for foxes.

"Well, Jennifer, this is a pleasure. We've heard so much about you. Welcome."

Adam took Jennifer's jacket to the hall closet and hung it with his own.

"Where's Father?"

"Let's go down into the living room. I'm sure he'll join us soon. You know how Wright enjoys his entrances. I've got some orange juice to refresh you after your little hike."

True to form, Adam thought, he'll appear just after we all get settled with glasses in our hands.

They arranged themselves in the living room. Hannah poured the juice into three glasses. Adam took two, gave one to Jennifer and sat down. Jennifer found the room self-consciously appointed with three tables covered with family pictures framed in silver but bereft of any sign of regular use, the atmosphere stale, almost oppressively so. A show room, she decided, the kind of thing she'd heard about but never actually sat down in.

It was time, Adam thought, based on experience, for his father to appear. Wright did not disappoint. As if conjured up by the thought, there he stood at the entrance to the living room, surveying the scene. With all eyes upon him, he descended the three steps to join the group, as Hannah announced, "Here's the Professor, coming to join us."

Wright was dressed in gray slacks, prominent belt, white shirt and tie and a Harris Tweed sport coat in the upper pocket of which a pipe protruded.

Jennifer and Adam rose and Adam said: "Father, I'd like to introduce Jennifer."

Jennifer extended her hand to meet Wright's, who said as he gently squeezed her hand: "I don't think I got Jennifer's last name."

"Stultz, Mr. Hudson. Jennifer Stultz."

"Please, sit down. I will join you with a glass of orange juice. Is 'Stultz' a Central European name?"

At the question, Hannah blanched. Looking hard at her husband for an instant, she then averted her eyes from everyone in the room, staring hard at her glass, as if to shatter it. Adam's face reddened. Unruffled, Jennifer replied, her voice calm.

"It's a Jewish name. My parents fled Poland for England just before the Nazis invaded. They later reached the United States, where they settled in the City before finding our present house in Mamaroneck. We are Conservative Jews."

Hannah said: "We have a number of Jewish friends, and, of course, at Columbia Law School, many of the faculty are Jews. Isn't that true, Wright?" Her voice implored him to take her shovel, lest she continue digging in the hole he had created.

Adam was mortified. With dread, he realized, the evening was just getting started.

They finished their drinks and went into the dining room. Hannah sought Adam's help in putting food on the table. Conversation proceeded, as usual in the Hudson household, with Wright acting both composer and conductor, with questions designed by him and directed by him to the person expected to respond. While the others tip-toed with caution in what they had to say, Wright appeared to be oblivious to the ripples of discomfort caused by his question in the living room, ripples that remained palpable in the dining room.

"And what, may I ask, is your father's employment?"

"He's a bookkeeper with Dyke Lumber. And my mother stays at home, caring for my two younger brothers and me. She studied piano with hopes of a career in music. Marriage and family ended that idea."

Father turned the conversation to the upcoming Presidential election.

"We're for Eisenhower. We voted for FDR, but now it's time for change. Stevenson's too professorial, a role I know. We anticipate a landslide. What's the thinking in your family?"

"Well, we've been Democrats since coming to America. My parents loved FDR. They liked Truman as well. Dropping the bomb, ending the war and all. They even predicted he could win against Dewey. They thought Truman had guts. They're for Adlai."

Adam said, "I agree with Jennifer on Truman. His defense of his daughter's singing was gutsy, as well as being funny. Someone at school told me he had an excellent record as an artillery officer in WWI."

By the time dessert was served, with Sanka, Adam believed they had survived the evening, at least since the initial shock in the living room. He could see from Hannah's relaxed expression that she too felt the worst was behind them.

"So, Jennifer, how are your grades?"

"Oh, Mr. Hudson, that's not my strong suit. My grades are average."

"I see. I suppose with athletics and the social life, you don't have time to apply yourself to your studies."

"Father, I don't think this kind of questioning …"

"It's okay, Adam. I can handle the question. Actually Mr. Hudson, I work hard on my studies. It got me passing grades, but nothing more."

"I see. Well, one can't expect to be good at everything. What do your parents think?"

"They know how hard I pushed myself. Often they urged me to take more of a break. And then my Dad told me that grades don't measure judgment. He said in life, judgment and a good footing in values are more important than grades. He said I was good in both, and my goal should be to hold on to that. He gave me self-confidence.

Adam claimed the last thought for the evening: "Your Dad got it right. On both points, you're an A plus."

❧

Reflecting on the evening, Adam didn't have to wait long to hear appraisals from his parents. Hannah spoke to him as soon as he had returned from walking Jennifer home.

"Jennifer's a peach. I liked her relaxed manner, her spunk. I saw a certain graciousness from beginning to end, without being self-consciously so. I suspect It's natural, something she isn't even aware of."

Wright had a couple of telephone calls to make just as Adam and Jennifer were leaving, and wasn't finished with them until after Adam had returned to hear his mother's warm words.

Wright appeared in the foyer to hear Adam say, "Mother, I think your reading of her is dead-on."

"I think your mother and I need to put our heads together before we give Jennifer a grade for the evening. You know, we always confer before expressing an opinion on matters like this. So let's sleep on it for now."

"Yes, Father. There are dishes to do. Mother, I'll join you in the kitchen."

At breakfast the next morning, Wright delivered what he described as a "parental perspective" on the subject of Jennifer Stultz. Wright was drawn to alliterative expressions, delighting in them even where their usage might be thought tasteless.

Looking at his mother's pained face, he knew the perspective was his father's alone.

"Jennifer's a fine girl. Unpretentious, serious, thoughtful—all that. But, simply stated, her tribe is not our tribe. With different history, customs and beliefs. You might think none of this matters, but our experience tells us it does. I've seen it many times over at Columbia. The differences might be suppressed at first, but in time they would surface to wound, if not destroy, your relationship with her. Tribes co-exist by keeping their distance. Jennifer should remain your friend. Nothing more. Do you agree?"

Adam suppressed the anger welling up inside. "Well, I'm not sure there's a choice. I feared you'd be put off by her lack of social standing and family affluence, compared to us. But your concern is that the family is Jewish. Isn't that, how to say, something close to what the Nazis thought?"

Hannah looked away, a drawn and anguished expression around her mouth and eyes, a fear of what might come next.

Wright jumped on the question, determined to stamp it to death as he might an ant scurrying across his newly swept kitchen floor.

"Of course it's not, Adam. You know better than to ask. There's not a racist bone in my body. Nor your mother's either. Recognizing tribal differences doesn't make one a racist. It simply makes one observant. Observant and cautious about life's big choices. Like marriage. Our home harbors no racists. Now, off to school with you. I'm glad we see eye to eye."

On the way to school, Adam rehearsed all that his father had said. Without a doubt, Wright had long experience with what he called tribal differences. Adam wished he could prove him wrong. What was "racism" if not the unthinking rejection by one tribe of another, on that ground alone. Isn't that what his father had just done? From experience, Adam knew it would be impossible to revisit this subject; he couldn't prove him wrong for, as far as his father was concerned, the subject was closed.

Adam continued his friendship with Jennifer through the last year of high school. He was her friend, and she his date, for dances, parties and outings. The relationship was warm but purely platonic. He liked "going steady" with Jennifer and did so despite pressure from his father, mostly subtle but on occasion not so subtle, to "play the field," broaden his female relationships, avoid such an early "commitment," as Wright put it. Adam was able to deflect his father's argument by reminding him that he had given full sanction to friendship with Jennifer. Although Wright never repeated the reasoning that they were from different "tribes," that argument was always at the front of Adam's mind whenever the subject of girls came up.

The Hudsons were friends with the Gordon family, who lived nearby in a large colonial house that the Gordons had lavished money on to modernize while preserving the aged expression of a house built in the 18th Century. Elliot Gordon was an investment banker at Morgan Stanley and Sally Gordon was involved in mothering their three daughters, maintaining the homestead, seeing to appointments with doctors and dentists, and keeping all fed and happy. She also was in a bridge club and did community service whenever a need appealing to her sense of fairness came to her attention. She preferred to wait until asked rather than to volunteer.

Elliot had graduated from Columbia Law School and embarked on a legal career at Reese, Mueller, but he quickly tired of what he referred to as "the exquisite attention to detail" that seemed to dominate the work of a young associate. He wanted to use his robust personality and facility with numbers in more remunerative ways. Investment banking seemed the answer, so after one year of misery at Davis Pearce, he solicited and then accepted an entry level offer from Morgan Stanley.

The eldest Gordon daughter, Robin, attended Miss Porter's School in Farmington, Connecticut. "Farmington" was an exclusive girls prep school with pretensions of importance equal to, or even greater than, those of Groton, the Massachusetts prep school for boys from which such aristocrats as FDR had emerged. Wright envied the means that the Gordons had to afford a prep school. The salary of a law professor made private high school education a reach. Of course, as Hannah more than once had observed to her husband, it came down to priorities, and Wright was, foremost, a devotee of sailing. To feed this appetite, he had dedicated savings to buy a vintage wooden sloop, one lovingly preserved in top condition, belying its age. The family used it to cruise the Atlantic coastline. Adam grew up loving to sail, and his attachment to the boat, in Wright's mind, justified the tradeoff he had made. But for this sailing extravagance, with all the expenses of upkeep, he would have sent Adam to Exeter, believing its size assured less exclusivity than a place like Groton, while offering a first-rate education. However, he was satisfied with the local high school, which had good teachers, good curriculum and enough smart, motivated students—a "critical mass,"—as Wright described this group—to assure Adam of ample scope and opportunity. The school also had a good record of placing top students in first-rate colleges.

Wright's frustration over Adam's steady relationship with Jennifer grew with the passing of the fall semester of his senior year. Robin Gordon was home from Farmington for Christmas.

Desperate to break up the Jennifer connection, or at least weaken it, Wright and Hannah decided to expose Adam to Robin, who was, like Adam, a senior. While some might see homeliness, Robin had a good figure, beautiful hair, a sophisticated mien that included a touch of *noblesse oblige*, and some other points impressive to Dwight, enough in his opinion to promote her to his son. The Hudsons invited Robin and her parents to dinner, asking them to pick an evening when their younger daughters could be otherwise occupied. The Gordons thought the idea rather gauche but, appreciating the desire to bring Adam and Robin together, they let the request pass without comment and found a suitable evening.

The initial tension created by the arrival of the Gordons soon dissipated with the help of martinis, straight up, for the adults and white wine for Adam and, as Wright put it, "Adam's guest Robin."

At dinner, Wright kicked off the evening by asking Robin what courses she was taking. He hoped the subject would have legs strong enough to carry the party through dessert.

Speaking in a high nasal voice that sounded to Adam like one practiced in taking on airs, Robin said: "American history from the Civil War to World War II, Great American Writers, covering Melville, Hawthorne and Lewis, and Calculus, Biology and Latin."

"Lewis? Oh, Sinclair Lewis. Quite a shift down from the other two. And what's your favorite subject?"

"I don't have a favorite. But I despise Latin. Not my strong suit. And why, anyway, should I have to learn a language long dead and buried?"

Adam said: "Father could explain the importance of Latin to anyone seeking to write or make his way with words. The roots of our language are mostly Latin. Perhaps your teacher wasn't too effective."

"That's an understatement. He tortured us. We read Caesar in Gaul. Each day in class we had to recite, reading out loud first the Latin and then our version of an English translation. Itchy Dawson, the teacher—that's what we called him outside class because he was inclined to scratch himself in front of the class—would grade us on each recitation with a simple plus or minus. Nothing in between.

At the end of each week he would rearrange the seating to put the student scoring highest in the last seat of the last row and then sort the rest according to scores. The lowest scoring student was in the front row, at the end. I often held that seat."

Hannah said: "How humiliating. And cruel."

"Do you study a foreign language, Adam?" Robin said, eager to shift attention somewhere else.

"Yes, French and Latin. Excellent teachers in both. I thought I needed to keep going with these two for a good shot at college. What are your plans for next year?"

"I'm applying to Bennett. I prefer a two-year college. Want to get all that behind me, go to the City, join the Colony Club and look around."

Adam could see from the expression on his father's face that his interest in sparking some attraction between Robin and himself had evaporated with the void his father saw in Robin's range and ambition. Adam had reached this conclusion ahead of his father, less on intellect than style and judgment. He was turned off by the nasal voice, the "to the manor born" mien, and the jewelry Robin wore, consisting of earrings of pearl set in a circle of diamonds and a necklace of richly crafted jade that reached the divide of her breasts, which were covered by a V-necked blouse revealing the absence of any bra. Too much glamour for his taste. As he later heard from a college friend who knew the prep school set, Farmington girls were famous for having begun the no-bra trend, which quickly became the daring and sophisticated thing to do, especially for those endowed enough for it to make a difference.

The Gordons looked on as the conversation progressed. Elliot was embarrassed by his daughter's description of her post-college plan, which, heard for the first time, surprised him. He feared it might be read as an intention to just hit the City in search of a husband. Sally knew that to be precisely the thing—or at least one big thing—that Robin had on her mind. Perhaps that's all she meant to be looking around for, or perhaps there were other things, like a job, a place to live, friends, etc. Robin didn't elaborate and her parents were unnerved by the statement, unwilling to chance probing further.

To change the subject Elliot turned to Wright.

"How are your students this term? Did you know that I'm a graduate, years back."

"I'm delighted to learn that. Did you practice before becoming an investment banker?"

"One year at Reese, Mueller. Couldn't take the detail work they piled on my desk. The experience felt like brushing my teeth with a file. I was lucky to escape. Investment banking has been good for me."

Hoping to leave even further behind the fraught atmosphere that enveloped the table after Robin's comment, Hannah joined the conversation.

"So, maybe you can explain the main difference in those professions? They seem like two peas in a pod to me."

"Fair question Hannah. I'd say the big difference is that at the law firm, they opine on the law and suggest options, but always leaving the hard decisions to their clients. At Morgan, Stanley, we make those hard decisions, or lead our clients to reach them. Another way of saying it: we take responsibility, ownership if you will, of the decisions our client must make."

Adam found Elliot's answer intriguing. He was more inclined to accept his mother's idea than Elliot's claims.

"Don't the lawyers have to '"take ownership,"' as you put it, for their legal opinions and advising on what will work within the law?"

"Why, Adam, to be sure, they do. But those opinions seldom plumb the heart of the matter. There are financial, political and social issues, all bearing on the business decision. The real risks typically are found in that decision, and that's the one the banking firm's hired to make."

The evening ended without further tension. As Wright ushered the Gordons out the front door and turned on the outdoor lights, he knew there was a definite, yet unspoken, feeling on the part of the Hudson household that Robin was not the girl for Adam. But Hannah ventured to ask Adam what he thought.

"Cosseted at home; privileged at school. Not my cup of tea, Mother."

Although the Robin gambit didn't pan out for Wright, something beyond his control reduced to the vanishing point his concern with the Jennifer connection. Jennifer, it turned out, was headed not for college following graduation, but the work force.

"No, Father, she's not going to accept that offer from Cornell. Her dad had a stroke. He's somewhat paralyzed in his arms. Had to give up his job. Her mother has her hands full with two boys in grade school and now, her husband to care for. Jennifer's going to try to help things by generating some income."

With Adam at Princeton, exposed to so much, including a social life that involved importing college girls to the all-male campus on weekends, Wright was confident that Jennifer would migrate from girlfriend to friend by the end of freshman year, if not before. Perhaps even to the forgotten list. "We needn't have worried," he told Hannah.

♼ 8 ♽

1955-1959

In June of Adam's freshman year, Wright summoned his son to his office for a review of the Princeton experience.

From Adam's viewpoint it had been a wonderful year. On the recommendation of his father, who believed it would be best for his ability to concentrate on studies to live alone, he'd asked for and got a single room in one of the large dormitories. This didn't seem to lessen the friendships he established. He made friends easily. His company was sought after, a "happy surprise," he told his father. He made the freshman swimming team and was admitted to the Nassoons for a tenor position, the group evaluating his voice as having more potential than he would have thought. The Nassoons were an elite choral group famed for its five- and even six-part harmonies and its gloriously amplified singing under Blair Arch. He loved his courses, particularly English 101, which was devoted entirely to Shakespeare and taught by a vintage professor, bearded white with hair askew and energy enough to act out choice parts in many of the plays they studied. He was, among Adam's friends, a "hoot," fitting perfectly a caricature of the classic Shakespearian scholar. Adam also found Economics 101 interesting. His particular way of thinking seemed well suited to economic analysis, which came easily. He'd decided to major in the subject. His grades, while falling short of his father's expectations, were satisfactory to him.

"From the sounds of all that you've said, I think we got our money's worth for the big tuition check I wrote. Here's how I see it. You had a good year, that's clear enough. You've met many interesting people. And you've grown up in almost all ways except scholarly achievement. The swimming and singing took more of your enthusiasm and attention than your studies. Time to turn that around next year. Overall, I congratulate you on a satisfactory start."

Despite having earned a B average for the year, Adam felt his father had given him a C. Not exactly a star to stick on his door.

In the winter of sophomore year, Adam and his classmates entered "The Bicker," a venerable process in which the eating clubs seek out those sophomores they want to invite to join their clubs. It is a selective process, and since those invited by at least one club include from 80 to 95 percent of the class, it is a cruel process for those few students left out. As perceived by the sophomores, there was a pecking order to the 17 or so clubs, with Cap and Gown, Cottage, Tiger Inn, Ivy and Colonial considered the most desirable by many students, and of course those clubs, themselves.

Adam found himself in demand. He was bickered by Cap and Gown, Cottage and Ivy. Apparently they all had swimmers and singers who made strong cases for Adam. Flattered by the attention, and somewhat pleased with himself, he told his parents of the decision that loomed ahead. He wanted them to know how well he was doing in what was a form of competition. And to get their advice, although neither had ever set foot in a Princeton eating club or knew much about them.

Adam explained the Bicker, ending up with a prideful opinion: "The clubs I have offers from, by all accounts, are among the most elite."

Hannah said: "How wonderful. To have such a 'high class' decision to make."

"I was hoping to get some help from you both. The choice is hard. I've eliminated Cottage, because it's known mostly for parties and screw-up types. Both the other clubs have wonderful members and the eating and playing facilities are essentially the same. I think I'd be tipped one way or another if I knew who among my friends was going where, but finding that out may be tricky."

Wright said: "What functions do the clubs serve beyond putting food on the table?"

"Well, that's where most of our social life takes place. For the last two years of college."

"That's precisely what I was afraid of. A place for partying. My strong advice to you is to stay clear of Cap and Gown and Ivy. Or any other club. You've already achieved the distinction of top-flight offers. You can dine out on that alone over the next two years. The fact is your scholarly results are not what we expected of you. Joining a club will make it doubly difficult to improve your academic performance—which is why we sent you to Princeton. I will not force you to reject these offers, but I urge you to do so. I know you are ambitious about academics, and if you think you can achieve outstanding grades while being in a club, so be it. That's a decision you can make, although I advise against it."

"Thanks Father. I gather you've given me enough rope to hang myself."

"Yes, that's the message, more or less."

If he had a tail, Adam thought, on returning to his room, it would be tucked out of sight. Opening up to his parents with warranted pride in the options open to him, with a request for help in choosing, his father's response had been to trample on his son's spirit until that pride was wrung out. What was it about the clubs that so bothered his father? For he could see Wright held deep, visceral feelings about the system, its selectivity and ranking. The Montana boy, who attended college and law school in Montana before flowering with a Circuit Court clerkship and an entry level teaching post at Columbia Law, had, with towering ambition and the grit of a loner determined to show the world, made it in New York City as a professor of law and penetrated the very center of what's considered 'the elite.' And, yet, the clubs offended him.

Adam feared it might be a case of one elite jealous of others, even to the point of despising them.

Adam found it easier than expected to discover the intentions of his friends. A group of them came to him, urging that he go with them to Cap and Gown. While celebrating the charms of Cap and Gown, they scooped up handfuls of mud to fling at Ivy. The silver candle sticks that never seem to tarnish, the candles that never seem to burn down. The white-only waiters. The creepy weed covering the walls. The preposterous pretensions. And, the coup de grace, Fitzgerald's comment in *This Side of Paradise* that Ivy attracted only "the detached and breathlessly aristocratic." Adam liked Fitzgerald. He knew he didn't fit the Ivy mold. But he wanted to be part of the club scene. He quickly decided to join his friends, putting his father's advice aside on the theory that he would achieve the good grades that Wright expected of him while enjoying his friends at Cap and Gown. After all, he reasoned, there were a number of juniors and seniors at that club who were candidates for *phi beta kappa*. And even more important to Adam, only a few who were featured in the Social Register.

In the spring of junior year, Adam met Elizabeth Stuart. A junior at Smith College, she had journeyed from Northampton, Massachusetts at the invitation of Bayard Throckmorton, a Social Register sort from Philadelphia, who had grudgingly joined Cap and Gown when his hopes for Ivy had vanished. Adam knew him enough to believe that Throckmorton must have fitted too precisely the Ivy mold Fitzgerald conjured up for even its own members to stomach.

It was May first, and the clubs were alive with party weekend energy and excess. Cap and Gown's managers had gone all out in booking a Lester Lanin band for the dance Saturday night. Adam had never heard of the Lanin band. One of the managers, bursting with enthusiasm, explained what a coup it was to have this band. "Lanin's a top bandleader. Really a class act. Much in demand. Famous for smooth tones, swift changes—elegant style with continuous music—Dixieland, swing, even rock and roll. If you like to dance, you're going to be very happy."

Adam came to the evening without a date. By happenstance, he took the last empty seat at the dinner table occupied by Bayard and Elizabeth, Bayard's roommate, Oliver Wooley, and his date. Bayard came to the table drunk. Elizabeth was forced, due to Bayard's incoherent mumblings, to engage Adam in conversation, a feat made easy by the discovery that they both sang. Elizabeth was a member of the Smiffenpoofs, a group, she explained, that was the oldest women's collegiate a cappella group in the country. In fact, the group had joined the Nassoons earlier in the fall for a joint performance at Princeton. It had occurred just before Adam was admitted to the group.

"I lost the chance to meet you last fall. I don't often get second chances. My lucky night," Adam said, a coy expression lining his face. With his roommate incoherent, Oliver realized the quality of Liz's evening was going to depend on Adam.

"Liz, you're sitting next to our Club's foremost declaimer of poetry. He is known on occasion to stand up at dinner and regale us with a poem. Do you feel the spirit move you now, Adam?"

"What sort of poem?" Liz asked, directing the question to both men.

"I like Kipling. But, especially, Robert Service. Do you know his stuff?"

"Not one I know. What did he write?"

"He was a Scotsman who came to Western Canada and became a cowboy. He became known as the Bard of the Yukon. His most famous poems, from his book, *Songs of a Sourdough,* are "The Shooting of Dan McGrew" and "The Cremation of Sam McGee." Perhaps, someday, I'll recite them for you. But not now."

Looking at Bayard, Adam could see that his drunkenness was growing more apparent to everyone at the table except Bayard, who continued to consume the red wine in front of him. Talking to Liz, his pleasure was enhanced by considering his sobriety in contrast to Bayard's drunken loss of control. As often happens, he began to feel superior to, and then pity for, the date who brought Liz to table.

By the end of dinner, when the Lanin Band began what seemed endless dance music, Bayard was unconscious. Oliver had enlisted a couple of club-mates to move him into the club library, where he could dry out on the deep carpeted floor. With the thoughtfulness of those who have been in Bayard's condition, both with respect to him and to the carpet, they put a bowl nearby for him to use, if necessary.

Thus did Adam succeed to the pleasure and responsibility of a date for the evening. Adam knew how to dance. Trained at the local dancing school during eighth grade, where he had to wear white gloves and bow deeply to each partner he danced with through rotation, Adam showed natural rhythm in gliding across the dance floor, whether to the beat of a waltz, fox trot, tango or rumba.

Elizabeth too had been trained in ballroom dancing. With practiced grace, she followed his lead from one tune to another in Lanin's continuous repertoire, beginning with Cole Porter's *From this Moment On.*

"Don't they take a bathroom break?" Elizabeth said, whispering loudly in Adam's ear.

"Beats me. Endless music is the Lanin trademark. Pee in their pants? No, they must take turns."

"I love this music. It makes me feel like I'm bouncing on clouds," Elizabeth whispered.

They danced and sat and danced some more and sat some more and suddenly the evening was over. No one had tried to cut in. Somehow, through the evening, he had learned Elizabeth's story, or Liz's as she asked to be called. Like Bayard, she came from Philadelphia and had been embedded in the Social Register along with the rest of her family. She had gotten to know Bayard at the many debutante parties that dominate the young social scene for the upper classes in this city of brotherly love. Bayard was just a friend, she said, but she knew, despite her discouraging signs, that his determined ambition was to migrate to romance.

"He pursues that goal in a somewhat strange manner," Adam said.

Liz said she was a joint major in Art History and American History. "My favorite painter is Hieronymus Bosch. Do you know his works? The best is *the Garden of Earthly Delights*, a triptych."

"I've never heard of him. Sounds Dutch."

"Yes, or Flemish. But that painting hangs in the Prado. I've been to see it. So much to take in. Erotic, macabre. I think Bosch was a master of human emotion. Perhaps the world's first psychologist. Disguised as a painter."

Adam asked about Liz's family. "I have two younger brothers, both away at boarding school. My father's an engineer at DuPont and my mother's a homemaker. Also something of a community organizer through our church."

At some point, on the dance floor, Liz said: "And you? How about the girls in your life?"

"No one just now. Free and unencumbered." With misgivings, Adam misled her. But to explore the subject fully, he believed would require some mention of his dream life, dominated as it was by recurring dreams of the muscle-toned bodies of young men barely clothed. His dream-life was a platform on which, in privacy, he could safely render by picture rather than by word his delicate and unexpressed longings. In fact, he considered himself homoerotic. It was a word he had to go to the dictionary to uncover, after finding it applied to Thomas Mann in an essay he had picked up early last summer. Fascinated by this great writer, he turned first to Mann's short novel, *The Holy Sinner*. It turned him into a fan. His summer became a Mann binge. He read *Death in Venice* and loved it; then *The Magic Mountain*, which he found boring as he pushed himself to finish. But by then he was hooked on the man and his ambiguous sexuality. And he even began *Joseph and His Brothers*, Mann's massive masterpiece. As these thoughts flickered across his mind, he felt lucky they were held tight against leakage, even as his head and Liz's were often in contact as they circled the room.

The evening progressed. So too did the closeness of their bodies as they moved in synch with the music. As if prompted by Lanin's smooth rendition of Porter's *Cheek to Cheek,* their faces tightened against one another and Adam, growing erect, worried Liz might notice. Later, as the music continued and with it their dancing, he realized he could feel her firm breasts and made the obvious connection. And, then, he began to worry she might not notice.

He took her back to the Nassau Inn, saying good night with a kiss on the cheek, that being all she offered.

"Exams are looming large for me," Adam said. "Perhaps we could get together again, right after the term ends."

"I'd like that. Perhaps you'd come to Philly. Let's be in touch. Hey, I have a better idea. Come over tomorrow for breakfast here. I'm on a bus back to Northampton, but it doesn't leave until 10. How about 8:30?"

Returning to his dorm, Adam marveled at the conventions he'd just experienced, first on the dance floor and then saying good night at the Inn. A couple who hardly knew one another could without constraint press their bodies together while dancing, from cheeks to chests to thighs and all in between, arousing each other throughout the night, so long as the music played, and then, in saying goodnight, limit themselves to a kiss on the cheek. He found the contrast stunning.

Adam met her in the vestibule of the Inn.

"Hello, Adam. You look no worse for wear. Let's go into the dining room. Guess what? I got a call from Bayard this morning. He was contrite. Asked to join me for breakfast. I had to tell him I had a breakfast date and would be catching the bus. I think this little affair is over."

"I guess now you've cleared the decks for your next conquest." Adam smiled at her.

"If Bayard was a conquest, it was wholly accidental."

They sat at a table and ordered from the menu. The room's walls were paneled in aged wood, darkened from decades in place. That and the absence of windows created a cave-like feeling.

"This place is a little creepy."

"Yes, I know. So, what's new at Smith? I've never visited the place."

"It's a remote female society on a little hill in Northampton. But it attracts men like lilacs attract bees, but not just in Spring. It buzzes with Yalie blues and Crimsons. Now and then, even those wearing orange and black. Can't fathom what attracts them. Earlier this spring, Harvard played Princeton in rugby on one of our fields, instead of one of their own. Remarkable."

"I see. With so many Queens, how can the drones resist? I hope soon to join the cluster."

The coffee arrived in a thermos, followed by eggs, bacon and toast.

"So, last night we compared notes on singing. Today, something else. Any good courses?"

"I like one in Greek and Roman Culture. We read Edith Hamilton's *The Greek Way* at the start and then dove into Pindar and the dramatists, Aeschylus, Euripides and Sophocles. And, then *Anabasis*. I was captured by Ancient Greece. How about you?"

"I know very little about Rome or Greece. And never heard of *Anabasis*. Another gap someday to fill."

"Now that you've got me started, I just finished a paper on the Greek definition of happiness. Want to hear?"

"Why not?"

"'The exercise of vital powers along lines of excellence in a life affording them scope.' What do you think, in a word?"

"Humm. Freedom. That's the word that comes to mind. That, and uncertainty about what they meant by 'vital' and 'excellence.'" Those Greek pretensions soar. To me, happiness is simple things like finishing a delicious meal, finding the dishwasher empty or taking a long shower. A visit to a new restaurant."

"I agree. Clean sheets to crawl into. Okay, pretensions, check. But they had reasons. They defeated the Persians at Marathon and Salamis. These were really heroic victories. And then there's Xenophon's *Anabasis*. He tells the story of how 10,000 Greeks, who had joined Cyrus's Persian Army to defeat his brother, then on the Persian throne, made the difficult journey back to Greece—after Cyrus lost the battle. My professor called them 'the 10,000.'"

Adam glanced at his watch.

"I know you see me as stuck in the mundane of life. So, here's a mundane thought: Your bus leaves from Palmer Square in twelve minutes."

"Okay, I can see you think I got carried away. To be continued. And, I never said I found *you* mundane. Indeed, it would be heroic of you to accompany me to the bus stop."

Hanging over the Hudson family as summer approached was the question of what Adam would do. His summer activities had always been decided by the family, with Adam responding to Wright's request for ideas.

"Your grades remain unimpressive. I hope you will plan something this summer that exercises the mind more than the body."

"I'm actually thinking about tying the summer to my thesis topic, which is going to be an evaluation of self-regulation of the securities markets. I'd like to try for a job with one of the stock exchanges."

"Good idea. I think I can help in securing a job. Won't pay much, if at all. But the experience—worth it."

What Adam had kept to himself was the fact that Liz had secured a summer job at Sotheby's, where she would be placed in the Textile Department. He abandoned the plan to drive west with a buddy from Cap and Gown, just to look around. An idea that, he knew, would summon stern objection from his father.

Mid-June found Adam working at the American Stock Exchange, where he helped those responsible for regulation of the listed companies, and Liz at Sotheby's helping the Director of Textiles and Carpets prepare for what they claimed would be a block-buster auction in September.

Hannah was the first to sniff out the fact that Liz and Adam had become an item. Adam, who was commuting to Wall Street, mentioned at breakfast that he would be home late.

"What's up?" Hannah asked.

"Oh, I'm going to see *Caesar and Cleopatra*, at the Beekman."

"I remember seeing that. Claude Rains, wasn't it? And Vivien Leigh. Great film. Going with anyone?"

"Yes, as a matter of fact, a girl. Liz Stuart. I met her at a Cap dance this spring. Thought I'd mentioned her."

"I'm sure I would have remembered, dear. Honestly, there's no need to sound defensive. Tell me about her. Perhaps she should come to us for dinner."

"Please, Mother, don't go building this up. She's just a friend. I don't want Father interrogating her. She's a Junior like me. She goes to Smith. She lives in Philadelphia. She's staying at the Barbizon this summer and working at Sotheby's. Her father's an engineer at DuPont. I don't know what her mother does, beyond maintaining the household."

"Well, I hope you're not planning to keep us in the dark. We should meet her. Goodness knows there haven't been many girls in your life. Please make a plan to let us in on your secret."

Liz met Adam for dinner at Bottega, a stolid and unpretentious Italian bistro at 2nd and 70th, within walking distance of the Beekman, a few blocks south. They arrived within a minute of each other, just before their reservation at 7:30.

"I'm not known for being on time." Adam said.

"Not my rep either. But I didn't want to miss the movie." Liz laughed at her silly remark, knowing the feature didn't start until 9:45.

"More to the point, Liz, this is our first dinner out together," Adam said, suddenly looking owlish, his voice a lecturing tone. "I suspect neither of us wanted to blow it by being late. And, of course, in this city, using the bus or subway, one either arrives early or late—seldom on time."

Hearing himself, Adam's temple ached as he identified his father in what he had just said, and how he had said it. He wondered what she was thinking.

"Not only prompt but sober."

"I'm impressed, you can tell. I recall your last date, at Princeton—how he came to dinner."

They were seated in a back corner at a table for two, where the waitress handed them well-used menus and, for Adam, a wine list.

"And while on the subject, how about a bottle of Chianti? If we don't finish it, they'll put one of our names on it and hold for our next visit."

"That's a nice touch. You've been here before, obviously. So, what do they do well?"

"Antipasto's creative. Spaghetti with white clam sauce. Shall I order?"

Liz nodded tentative agreement. "Clams fresh, I assume." She took a deep breath, as if to indicate the time had come, at last, to relax.

"Right. Little necks."

"Now, tell me what you do all day? I know, you're preparing for an early September auction. What's involved?"

"I really lucked out in this job. I'm being paid to be taught about textiles. Actually, one in particular. A little-known art form from the mountains of Dagestan. Kaitag art it's called. Ever heard of it?"

"No. The only threads I know are the couple of Brooks Brothers suits I got for my summer on Wall Street. Dagestan—I think I can locate. Between the Black and Caspian. Are Kaitags a kind of rug?"

"No, they're weavings of silk, usually around two feet by four feet, colored with animal and vegetable dyes. Reds, blues, yellows. Not made for foot traffic or to cover dirt floors in the yurts. They were used in rituals associated with birth, marriage and death."

Adam's invitation unleashed the teacher in Liz, the exercise of which brought to her profound and often unstoppable pleasure, like digging into a pint of chocolate ice cream covered in pecans.

"When were they woven?"

"They appeared in the late 19th Century. And yet the images are abstract, very modern-like. There's plenty of mystery surrounding the people who created this art and the motifs found in the samples we will have on offer at the auction. Trying to scope out the meaning of the images is frustrating fun. If you know what I mean."

While Adam was concentrating on Liz's Kaitag story, the waitress had poured some Chianti into Adam's glass and was waiting, with growing impatience, for his approval.

"I think she awaits the routine," Liz said.

"With corrugated brow, Adam sniffed the cork, swirled the wine in his glass and breathed in the bouquet deeply, as he had seen his father do. He then took a sip from his glass and nodded with a dismissing flourish of his hand.

Liz didn't know how to read him. Pretentious or just pretending.

"Can you describe a Kaitag?"

For Liz this was an invitation to become didactic.

"You'll get the idea if you come to the auction. But I'll try to describe a design I've spent a lot of time on. It's a cosmic map, or actually a symmetrical pair of maps facing each other. There's a central tree of life climbing up to an umbrella-like layer of heaven. The tree is flanked by a pair of serpents, which I've learned, are symbols of the connection between earth and heaven. Here, give me your pen and I'll try to sketch it on this napkin. Drawing's not a strength."

"They're woven on looms?"

"Oh, I should have mentioned the technique. A loom is used to create the cotton ground cloth. Then the design is created, typically free-hand, in silk embroidery, using something called a couch stitch. Don't know why. I'm in the process of learning about that stitch and the others used in these textiles." Liz looked at her drawing and, knotting her temple, crumpled it up in a ball.

"Enough about me. How's your job working out?"

The antipasto arrived, invoking a tiny spurt of pleasure for Liz to replace the embarrassment of having lectured to long. On her plate black and green olives hobnobbed with red peppers and purple onions, while a sea of anchovies settled on a bed of genoa salami and creamy provolone. The tubed bottle of first press olive oil that the waitress had left them seemed redundant, but just in case, she anointed her plate with a couple of shakes' worth.

Adam refilled their wine glasses.

"Wall Street is something else. It has its own unique smells, a blend of swagger and sweat, combined with the odors of street vendor grills—a mix of chestnuts, hotdogs and onions, and the morning fresh offerings of fishmongers. Streets streaming with people, mostly men, moving fast, self-contained and self-important, oblivious to surroundings, morning papers tucked under arms, bent over with purpose, as if the world would crash and burn without them."

"Fishmongers! I keep forgetting how close Wall Street is to the docks. Is the pace and all thrilling?" Liz asked, reaching out to stroke Adam's wrist with her fingers, while offering a quick wink of her right eye. He wondered if this was a habit of hers. He had noticed it once before. Her timing surprised him. She had triggered a ripple down his spine, perhaps equaling the pleasure Liz got from the antipasto.

"Thrilling? Yes, but not for much more than an instant. I don't feel part of the game. Still just a spectator."

"But how about the Exchange? Your work?"

"Ah, that's different. Once I enter the Exchange and sit down at my desk, I feel I belong. It's a friendly, joke-ready place, with plenty of laughs to ease the work—to grease the frictions, if you know what I mean."

"Hey, that's my phrase. And I do know what you mean. Laughter's the best way to get through the day. We laugh a lot in textiles. Especially over jokes, usually told by a woman who learns new ones every day from her husband, who, she claims, is an extremely horny trader at the Stock Exchange. She says he picks up raunchy jokes like a cat licks up spilt milk."

"If Wall Streeters devoted as much imagination to trading as they do to creating jokes, they'd all be rich enough to quit. But about my job. Well, for starters, I'm at the bottom of the heap. I handle a lot of paper. I fetch coffee for my boss. I'm lucky he doesn't ask me very often. I do whatever they ask. But my main job is processing the filings that public companies submit in order to register with the Exchange and have their debt and equity securities traded. Nothing exciting happens until a company is caught by the financial press in some wrong-doing. Then the filing becomes important, and I get involved with others in trying to dope out whether the filing was fraudulent. The best I can do is try to find ways to be useful."

The main course was served. The waiter offered the famed Parmigiano, grated at table with a large circular grater. Looking down his prominent nose to the cheese shards below, Adam gestured to the waiter for more. "I can't get enough of this cheese. How about you?"

Liz reddened slightly, too tiny a tinge for Adam to notice, even in a well-lighted space, which their corner certainly was not.

"When you first mentioned this cheese, I hadn't a clue. Then, when the waiter offered to grate 'the Reggiano,' I caught on. As for liking it, I have no idea. But, in a minute or two, I'll let you know. I bet the cheese is named for some town in Italy."

"Yes, in Tuscany."

"And the clams, for a town on Long Island?" Liz's mischievous smile melted into laughter before Adam caught the joke. Reddening, he tried to catch up.

"If you like, why not?" Adam said, a grimace tensing his chin and lower lip.

☙❧

It was a short walk from the Beekman, at 3rd and 59th, to the Barbizon, at Lex and 63rd. On the way, Liz explained that the Barbizon was the only women-only resident hotel in the City. "A lot of movie stars stay there; it's considered a safe retreat, although I doubt the likes of Rita Hayworth came to avoid lust-crazed admirers. I'd like to invite you to my room, but the rule is no men above the lobby. I've heard a handful have made it past the clerks, but if caught they say you spend the night in jail."

"Instead of in the arms of your sweetie. Ouch!"

As they approached Lex on 63rd, Liz moved into an entrance-way to a closed store, taking Adam's hand to pull him with her.

"We best say goodnight here, if we want some privacy." That wink again. "The movie was all it claimed to be, and more. And the meal at Bottega—perfection. And all within easy walking distance. Adam, you plan well. If you'll permit me an encore, I'll try to pull something together and be in touch."

Squeezing his hand, she pulled his head down. She kissed him on the lips, lingering, Adam imagined, to assure herself. He was caught unawares, having, even before reaching the hotel's entrance, happily accepted Barbizon rules, because he thought they would relieve him of the stress of figuring how to bring the evening to a close. Pressed against his, her lips, unimaginably soft, felt good. Pulling back, he was about to describe his feeling when she pulled him down again, this time injecting her tongue to explore around his mouth and, finding his tongue, tease the tip of it. He accepted the now evident fact that she was practiced. And in charge. Had a policeman not come along, he wondered, how long would she had kept him there in the entrance way.

Walking to Grand Central after seeing her into the Beekman's lobby, he rehearsed his feelings. She'd intended to arouse him. He knew she'd succeeded. And yet. His body had responded, but his mind was uncertain. And relief cloaked him as he thought of the hotel rules.

Sitting opposite Adam, on the late train to Mamaroneck, was a young Asian. One could hardly describe him as anything but beautiful. Adam felt drawn to this man. Perhaps it was just the tailings from his arousal in the arms of Liz, but he became excited as he looked the man up and down, imagining the curve and heft of his lower body, his hairless legs, his slim beauty. He thought of ways to break through the silence between them, to engage. The man showed no interest in Adam, and while Adam knew how to open conversation with a stranger and was normally comfortable in doing so, something—a sense of danger perhaps—held him back from walking the thoughts held dark in his head step by step into the train's light.

The morning after Adam's date with Liz, when he arrived in the kitchen for a quick breakfast before dashing for the train, his parents buried him with questions about Liz. Although he had imagined inviting her to spend a weekend at their house, the freedom to do so was turned on its head, becoming for Wright and Hannah a son's duty to show and tell, to gain acceptance, before things got serious. Like two butterflies in heat, they fluttered about the subject of Liz, demanding a chance to meet her. Wright put their concern in upper-cased bold type by ponderously intoning: "IN THIS DOMAIN, A MISTAKE CAN BE FATAL." Looking back, Wright remembered his son had already made one mistake.

A weekend in August was picked for Liz to visit Mamaroneck. She'd come out on a train with Adam on Friday evening, in time for dinner, and return by train late Sunday afternoon, having sailed with Adam on Saturday and Sunday. Adam explained to her that his father was a keen sailor, member of the American Yacht Club in Rye and proud owner of a Herreshoff S Class Marconi rig wooden sloop. It was built in 1920 and named Doodah by its first owner. With Hannah's agreement, Wright had named it the Dorothy, for the daughter they never had.

"I've sailed a bit," Liz admitted to Adam on the train. "Mostly on a sunfish. I know my starboard from my port. But not much more. How big did you say Dorothy was?"

"20 feet, 6 inches on the water line; 27 feet, 6 inches overall. Beam 7 feet, 2 inches."

Like his father, Adam was precise in matters of sailing. He had been taught. And he had responded. Like his father, he looked for any sign of appreciation for his expertise, which he caught in Liz's expression.

"So we're going to sail tomorrow, rain or shine, wind or no. But where are we going to point your beautiful vessel?"

The conductor intervened, demanding tickets.

"We're together," Adam said. "Hope to go sailing tomorrow. How's the weather look?"

"Do I look like a weatherman? I heard there might be sun, or clouds or wind. Who knows? That's the size of it. Worth what you paid for." Chuckling, he moved down the aisle to the next passenger.

Adam's parents crowded the door to welcome Liz and Adam. Hannah took Liz to the guest room and left, saying dinner at eight with drinks before in the living room.

"No rush."

Liz sensed, before it was plain for her to observe, that this weekend was, if not a final exam, at least an important mid-term. Coming into the living room, in which Adam and his parents had already settled down, drinks in hand, Liz felt like a frog in biology class.

"What would you like, Liz?" Wright asked, sprightly. "We're having gin and tonic. But we have most anything on offer."

Curious. Liz wondered why Wright adopted that British expression.

"I'll join you with the gin and tonic. A little lime too, if you have it."

Liz had changed into a flowery cotton dress, embellished with a string of pearls of graded sizes that suggested age and value. What Hannah and Wright saw, when Liz paused a moment at the threshold to the living room, was a woman projecting casual confidence, comfortable with the setting, aware of being put on trial and open to the challenge. They saw a figure of height and distinct curves, a sculpted mouth, a nose, chin and cheekbones, each well-defined, and eyes deep-set and blue-green, etched against a background of light brown eyebrows and hair. Her eyes were unusually close to each other, giving her face a natural intensity and easy ability to make anyone she looked at believe she could focus only on him. Yet her concentrated attention was warm and open, flattering rather than threatening.

"Adam told us you are in the Textiles Department at Sotheby's. Did you want that assignment?" Hannah asked.

"In fact, I did. I put in a request and they honored it. Lucky turn of the wheel."

"I understand you're an art major at Smith. Is that the source of your interest in textiles?" Wright said.

"Actually I'm a joint major in Art and American History. My love for painting extends from the Renaissance down to Picasso.

I lose interest with the abstractions of modern expressionism. De Kooning, Pollock and the like. When I look at a masterpiece like Bosch's *Garden of Earthly Delights,* and consider the imagination and skill involved, and then contrast that extraordinary achievement with Jackson Pollock's dribbling of paint across a canvas lying on the floor beside his feet, I get turned off by what now qualifies as art. In applying to Sotheby's I was afraid they might send me to work on Pollocks—a fate worse than death, if you know what I mean."

"I can tell you've explained this before. But why textiles?" Wright asked, probing further, as if, Liz thought, he'd handed her a blue book and asked her to write about herself.

From experience, Adam knew his father was determined to press Liz as his ancient hero, Socrates, might have done to uncover whatever revelation might lay hidden, including the possibility that only emptiness crouched behind the opinion. The risk wasn't his and he took delight in laying it on students every day in his law school classes. Wright couldn't restrain himself from using on guests in his home precisely the same method he practiced on students at Columbia.

"Because I love them. But the why would take a bit of explaining. I don't want to monopolize the conversation."

"No problem." Rising, he said, "I think I'll have a splash more. Anyone else need their drink freshened? Now, please give us the why," Wright said, testing.

Watching the scene unfold, Adam went from alarm to the pleasure of realizing Liz was in the process of leading his parents on, ensnaring them in her web of science-based facts.

Again she took note of Wright's affectations. "This may sound like a lecture. Which may be okay because Professor Hudson is a practitioner. I appreciate textiles in many ways. The long-held idea that true art cannot be functional repelled me. I turned to textiles precisely because they are functional art.

"And, then, there's the matter of creating a textile. The Pazyryk, the oldest pile carpet in existence, was woven in the Iron Age, about 400 years before the birth of Jesus. It measured about six feet square. It would have consumed the wool of 100 sheep. After shearing, the wool would have to be dyed the many different colors to be used. Making the dyes, of vegetables and insects, was itself a demanding form of technical skill and art. By the way, they used urine to fix the colors. Then the loom would need to be prepared for weaving, followed by the tying of densely packed knots—the pile. Along the way, the weaver would have to create the design to be rendered on the loom. And then, finally, the weaving could begin. In the case of the Pazyryk, experts reckon that the weaver took two years to complete what is generally considered a masterpiece. So, there you have it. How can one not admire the art of weaving? At most, it leaves just scraps to applaud in Pollock."

Wright said "Fascinating." Hannah gushed. "Wonderful! You proved your case, Liz. Looking at the rugs we have around the house, I know they will seem shabby to you. I'm thinking I should go to the next Sotheby rug auction, while you're still there."

"That's a capital idea, Mrs. Hudson. I'll send you our catalog for the auction, when it's ready. We would love to see you there."

They went into the dining room for dinner. Adam could see that Liz had seduced his parents, assuring that the rest of the evening would proceed well. He was pleased with himself, recalling his parents' reaction to Jennifer. The conversation remained focused on Liz, bouncing from her early years with family in Philadelphia to sailing experiences, courses at Smith and Adam's plans for sailing down the sound to Stony Brook Harbor in Smithtown the next day, anchoring there and sleeping on board over-night. More observer than participant, Adam watched the evening unfold with the satisfaction of knowing he had pleased his parents. Like a little boy eating his spinach without prompting, or a young skipper earning kudos from his father for a timely tack.

The idea of Adam and Liz spending the night alone on the *Dorothy* appeared in the dinner conversation to be natural, unworthy of particular note. And, having got a sense of his parents, Liz was amazed. She knew her parents, laid-back as they were, if confronted with this plan, would have plenty to say before signing off. But Adam had had it out with Wright and Hannah the previous night. In fact, the parents were of two minds. Given Adam's limited showing of interest in girls other than as school companions, and as such, not as many or as close companions as the boys he hung around with, Hannah and Wright were delighted by the presence of Liz in his life and eager to be supportive. But sleeping on the same boat at their age? As they talked to Adam, he imagined the inner conflicts they might be feeling.

Wright summed it up. "We're not concerned with your getting ahead of yourself and getting Liz pregnant or anything like that. Not in the least. It's reputation. Our family reputation, your reputation, and Liz's, if people see you both, see what you're doing and start talking in the community. That's the issue. A Mrs. Grundy problem as it's known. On the other hand, we are delighted you are going to take the *Dorothy* for a spin around the Sound with a girl. On balance we'll take the risk."

Saturday started out calm and clear, but by the time Adam and Liz had hoisted sail, a brisk breeze from the Southwest had developed, with promise of growing stronger through the afternoon. Liz admired Adam's boat-handling skills. She could see he was extraordinarily self-confident in his ability to handle whatever might come along. It wasn't that he was puffed up or boastful. To the contrary, it was his quietness in wielding control of sails and tiller that radiated both the attitude of mastery and the underlying skills needed to support it. It occurred to her, with scorn, that sailboats from long ago must have been given female names by males skilled in handling them and playfully aware of the sexual counterpoint to the commonplace words they used to describe that skill. Watching Adam now, hair flowing and sun brightening half of his face, she felt a ripple of pleasure course through her body.

They sailed, they ate their sandwiches and drank their V-8, and, reaching Stony Brook Harbor, they anchored off the Yacht Club. The wind, which, as Adam predicted, had waxed through the afternoon, driving them forward in the comfort of a broad reach, dropped with evening to the mildest of breezes as a full moon rose in the East over Long Island. They had brought a dinner to be cooked on a portable gas stove. The evening passed quickly. They used sleeping bags and air mattresses to stretch out on the two benches in the Dorothy's cockpit. Liz wanted to lie with Adam, but the narrow bench meant she would have had to be on top of him and he had promised his parents they wouldn't do anything that would embarrass the family if seen from other boats or from shore. The full moon was bright enough to cast shadows. There were many boats in the harbor, making privacy in a boat without a cabin below decks impossible.

For Liz, disappointment over the absence of physical connection was made deep and acute precisely because of her rather grand expectations of what was in store for them on a private sailing adventure in a beautiful vessel, a full moon and perfect weather. She felt hung out to dry, with no one to blame except her vivid imagination, which had embraced the prospect of ending her virginity on board the Dorothy. She had brought along a newly fitted diaphragm. She wanted to tell Adam of her disappointment, but the certainty of feeling humiliated stopped her. How much worse she would have felt had she known of Adam's relief at not having to face Liz's expectations.

It was well after midnight when the tide reached heights in the Harbor rarely equaled, even on previous full moons. In setting anchor, Adam had ignored the moon's effect. He knew about the moon's effect on tides. And their effect on anchor lines. For whatever reason, he had just forgotten. With too little scope on the line, the rising tide gently lifted the anchor from the sandy bottom, freeing the Dorothy to move as current and wind might direct. A stronger breeze greeted the boat as it was released to drift. Adam awoke with the first collision. The *Dorothy* had hit a near-by yawl amidships and moved along the yawl's side until free, leaving behind touches of paint to mark the event. An angry voice came from below the yawl's deck. It took Adam but a minute and one glance at the moon, now high overhead, to realize his blunder. Looking in the direction the *Dorothy* was headed, he could see the next collision would be a breakwater of large rocks marking the entrance of the harbor. By now, Liz was awake.

He had found the long oar and was getting ready to fend off from the rocks. "Grab the tiller and steer us away from those rocks. See them to port. To point the boat away, to starboard—to the right—you move the tiller to the left."

She said: "Really? To the left?"

"Trust me, just do it. Quickly."

Responding to their coordinated efforts, just in time the boat swung starboard.

"The problem was the wind and my having only two hands. I had hoped to surprise you with a moon-light sail. Silly of me to try to handle everything myself. Sorry. But look, in a couple of hours, the sun will appear. We should be back at the *Dorothy's* mooring by noon."

"But did you lose control?"

Adam struggled for the right answer. He had been trained from diapers on never, ever, to lose control. For Wright it was the ultimate failure in character. Like heart failure but worse, because it was within one's power to address.

"Not really. I was going to wake you to take the tiller while I finished hauling the anchor, but the breeze came up a bit, and we had to be prepared to fend off the rocks. With your seamanship, it came out well."

"What happens now?" Liz's voice sounded anxious.

"Simple. You steer us out of the harbor, the wind luckily is pushing us from the south, while I finish with the anchor. Then I put up the sails and we begin the voyage home."

"Bathed in moonlight. Not bad at all."

The return to Rye was uneventful, except for the delight they found in the multiple wonders surrounding them: the beauties of the Sound and the *Dorothy*, jib and main taut and filled with a gentle wind now from the southeast, the lapping of waves, the moon's light slowly replaced by the dawn of another fair day and the pleasures they took in themselves and each other. The breeze salted their lips, and the sun, climbing overhead, baked their cheeks.

And yet. Each of them occupied a sealed bubble of thought. He couldn't avoid rehearsing, again and again, as they sailed toward Rye, the night's blunder and his inability to admit error to Liz. Or others, for he knew this had become a habit. Or call it a flaw. What gene, what nurture, made it impossible for Adam to say, as one might easily have done here, "Hey, Liz, I really fucked up. Forgot a full moon brings high tides." He knew this habit, better to call it a compulsion, couldn't be traced to genes alone. Wright had played a role.

Liz too kept pondering the incident, again and again trying to dismiss the likelihood that Adam was lying. The plan for a moon-lit sail sounded phony. She noticed the periodic cloud that crossed Adam's face, only to vanish before she could summon the courage to inquire. She felt something was off, knew in her bones it related to the night's adventure but found it too risky to confront, too much to her disadvantage, and, at bottom, too scary to push against Adam's story.

We like her. Adam, you've landed a keeper," Wright announced soon after Liz had left their home for the Barbizon, sounding as if he were reporting the results of a football game in which the underdog team had won.

"Father, I haven't 'landed' anything. Haven't even hooked anything—or even baited the hook. I know the use of metaphors is as necessary for you as breathing, but please don't make these assumptions. I mean, yes, we like each other, yes, we plan to see each other again, but that's about it. We just enjoy each other's company."

Hannah broke in. "Dear, all we mean is that, if you want to think of her as a girl-friend, we approve."

Wright said: "Indeed, my love, we encourage it."

While being pleased with their reactions, Adam pushed back. "Here's my thought. If the weekend had been in Philadelphia, with Liz's parents evaluating me, can you imagine her father saying to her, after I left, 'Liz, you've landed a keeper.' Not likely."

"Okay, Adam, you've squeezed all the juice you can from this lemon."

In October of 1958, their senior year, Adam traveled to Northampton for the long Columbus Day weekend. Their intimacies of the summer had grown more intense, frustratingly so because they found no opportunity to be safely alone. Arriving in Northampton on Friday afternoon, he met Liz in front of Talbot, her House. Getting in his car, she said they would go to a local inn to get Adam a room for the weekend. The parietal rules in Smith's Houses were extreme and vigorously enforced. Smith had no dormitories. Under the House Rules, male guests were allowed in the girls' rooms only on Saturdays from three to five in the afternoon. Doors to the rooms had to remain open and the rule was "Four on the Floor" at all times. To insure compliance, Housemothers patrolled the halls like prison guards warned of a planned breakout, seemingly eager to catch a girl in an act of romance the likes of which they could only imagine. Liz had no desire to introduce Adam to the rigors of intimacy attempted in Talbot, where the cry of "man on the floor" would identify a male dumb or bold enough to reach the second floor on a Saturday before 3 pm.

After securing the room, they left the inn, arm in arm. Without a word, both of them knew the booking would offer opportunities denied them over the summer. But not Friday night. Liz had faculty meetings that evening that could not be canceled or delayed.

On Saturday, the sky clear, the temperature crisp, the foliage magnificently adorned in bright yellow, orange and red against green, they met for breakfast and then biked to an apple orchard, where the fruit could be picked and cider pressed. Liz knew her apples. The orchard offered Winesap, Northern Spy and Ashmead's Kernel, all excellent for eating as well as for cider. They picked some of each, returned to the cider operation and offered their pickings to the cider-making machine—an ingeniously simple affair with the dual function of grinding and pressing, so that at least two operators could be set to work, and for efficiency a third to convey the apples to the grinder. In return for picking, customers were entitled to gallon containers of cider, in amounts proportionate to the number of apples picked.

They threw themselves into the exercise, taking over the cider machine and its grinding and pressing functions, getting themselves thoroughly covered with bits of apple leavings and juice. He said: "This reminds me of that scene in *Moby Dick* when the men are working the whale, hands buried in blubber."

"Yes, yes, a riveting moment, isn't it?" She placed her wet hand over his and squeezed. "Of course, all that latent homosexuality doesn't have much to do with us."

Adam recoiled, suddenly aware of his stupidity at having read Melville's masterpiece without even grasping the homosexual overtones. Why had that scene become etched in his memory? Unconscious awareness? Was he deceiving Liz? He wanted to speak to her of these things, but the deep uncertainties about who he was threw up an iron-like curtain.

She ran out of apples to grind, just as he ran out of unanswerable questions. Looking up at the sun, feeling the breeze, he forced his mind to switch gears, to rejoin the healthy plentitude around him.

They attended a dinner-dance that evening. Elvis, Buddy Holly and BB King alternated with slow melodies like *Moon River*, intended to encourage bodies to tighten and press against one another, head to toe. The intimacies of the day swelled with the music. Just after midnight, they drove through a chilly star-speckled night to the inn. Liz had checked out from Talbot, using the log to indicate she would be staying off-campus for the night.

"Liz, it seems at odds with Smith's rules in the Houses to allow you just to sleep anywhere you like just by signing out."

"Amazing, I agree. Smith's not known for consistency, especially in regard to males. But I think the point is responsibility, which they view as ending when a student goes off-campus."

The second-floor room Adam had rented was small and cold. The walls had what must have been ancient wall paper, faded where window light hit it and peeling in many spots. A radiator was on but offered no heat. There was a common bathroom serving two rooms. The bed was queen-size and appeared to have enough blankets to compensate for the lack of heat. Its springs were soft and squeaky. Liz said "Let me use the bathroom first. I will come back and tuck in under the covers. Then it'll be your turn."

A slice of Adam stood apart, fascinated by the proceedings, proceedings that seemed so perfectly shaped by Liz's hands, as if she were practiced in a routine so ordinary that she could manage it in her sleep. When she emerged from the bathroom, she found another guest waiting to use the facilities. Impatient but not unpleasant.

"You'll have to wait a minute. Some guy snuck in ahead of you." She took off her bright blue and white bathrobe, revealing herself to Adam in all her nakedness. He couldn't take his eyes off her, moving from the top down and then back up slowly. Liz was confident of her body with its Botticelli-proportioned limbs. And her pride, saved up in her mind for just this moment, expressed itself before Adam.

"Surely you've seen a woman before. You're looking at me like those Prado museum gawkers look at Eve in the Bosch triptych. They liked what they saw. Do you?"

With vigor, he nodded. In fact, he'd never before stood in front of a naked woman. The realization took him by surprise. The whole process was new to him, and to a degree frightening. Then, saved by the sounds outside their room of a toilet flushing and a door opening and closing, he said, "The coast is clear. I'll be right back."

He washed up, pulled out a razor from his shoddy toilet kit of leather, worn and dirty, and quickly shaved. Alas, too quick to avoid cutting his chin, just above the dimple. He washed away the blood, put a piece of toilet paper on the cut, took the anticipatory condom out of the kit and, palming it, returned to their room, with only a towel around his waist. Noticing that his preparations had given him an erection, Liz smiled. "I see that bathroom turned you on."

Liz was snuggling under a couple of wool blankets. "It's warm in this pool. Dive right in."

He dropped the towel. He put the condom on the bedside table. Then, pulling back the bedding, he lay down beside her. Liz, noticing the condom, said, "No need, I'm all set with a diaphragm."

Adam was a clinical paranoid about unintended pregnancy. Despite having never, until this moment, been in circumstances where he could impregnate a woman, it had always been a deep-seated worry.

"That's thoughtful. Really. But look. It isn't 100%. I mean nothing is. In something like this, I'm a belt and suspenders guy. I hope you understand."

From that point on, the evening seemed determined to descend, a slippery slope to disaster.

First, his erection shrunk as he tried to install the condom, creating at best a sizing problem.

Then, she devoted much time to restoring him to the robust condition with which he had entered the bed. The challenge was sharpened by his chin, which had resumed bleeding when the toilet paper fell off the cut. Liz used a shred of Kleenex to stop the bleed. Then she resumed, using hands, lips and tongue with skill, whether practiced or innate Adam didn't know and, in time, didn't care, finally achieving for Adam the objective of arousal, evidenced by what now could be called a well-tailored fit. In the course of her labor of love, lavished solely on Adam, she discovered, as numberless women had discovered before her, that what's sauce for the gander is sauce for the goose as well.

While admiring her handiwork, he worried. Would his erection, like a bulging balloon released of its air, collapse before use? He mounted her and entered. He moved in and out. Lasting less than a minute, he came, withdrew his now shriveled penis, rolled over and immediately fell asleep.

Abandoned, she used her hands to pleasure herself in the only sure way she knew how.

❧ 9 ☙

1959-1961

Adam and Liz stuck together. If questioned, neither would admit to being deeply in love. They were just comfortable together, as a couple, finding pleasure in each other's company. They saw one another almost by default, finding it so much easier to be with one whose pieces in the puzzle of life fit neatly with the puzzle of the other, or at least, with some of its pieces, were jointly seen as ill-fitting but worthy of work. Striking out to find someone new would have meant, for Adam or Liz, overcoming inertia, and experiencing dissatisfaction with the other beyond compass, something not on the horizon. By the time Adam entered law school in the fall of 1959, they were like broken-in shoes, still new enough to have a long life ahead but worn enough to have carved comfort by smoothing the rough spots.

Adam had done well on the LSAT, in the 93rd percentile. He applied to Yale, Harvard and Columbia. All three accepted him. Advised by Wright, who saw a conflict at Columbia, given his professorship, and who thought Yale more enthused with social policy than the law, Adam was guided toward Harvard.

She found a job at the Gardner, working in the art restoration department. Although she knew next to nothing about restoring paintings, the stunning recommendation letter from Sotheby's opened one of the Gardner's doors, and her placement simply responded to need. She considered the job an elite opportunity, not to be missed just because the work offered was unfamiliar.

They lived together on Bryant Street in Cambridge, within walking distance of law school and subway. A third-floor suite of living room, bedroom, bath and kitchen was rented out by an empty nesting couple, and they had found it not in the advertisements, but by walking this secluded, tree-lined street, knocking on doors. Luck parading as audacity and perseverance.

Liz heard Adam's footsteps, ascending to their suite after his first day's classes. She gave him a hug at the door. "How'd it go?"

"In a word, intimidating. Professors and students seem so damn smart, so articulate."

"Come into the kitchen. I just made some coffee. I may have told you my father, long ago, lasted at Harvard for one year, before realizing his future was Engineering. On the first day, the Dean told the class: 'Look to your left and look to your right. At least one of those you see won't be with us next year.' Dad felt a certain lack of warmth in the good Dean's welcoming comments. I'm sure that dreadful practice has disappeared."

"Yes. Dean Griswold was, if not warm and cuddly, at least welcoming of all of us, and threatening to none. His opening remark was 'My name is Griswold. I'm the Dean of this place.' He said we would be 'journeymen lawyers acting as lubricators in our society.' He denied any school policy to arouse scholarly competition but sought a tradition of excellence. What's interesting is our class of 532 includes just a handful of women."

"And Negroes?"

"I think only two."

There was another statistic Adam wondered about but kept to himself. The number of students who were homosexual. And the number of professors, for all of them, Adam had noted, were men. He knew one student in his class who was very likely of that persuasion. Henry Wolfson, his swimming friend from Princeton, had entered the law school in Adam's class. They had remained friendly after the incident in the pool, and joined the same four-person study group at Harvard, but, despite this waxing friendship, they were not close enough to have discussed each other's current sexual life. Adam had sensitive antennae for the homosexual frequency, and they tuned into Henry when he greeted Adam in Austin Hall just before the Dean spoke.

"Adam Hudson. Good to see you. Hadn't known you were coming to Harvard. Am I correct in assuming you're married … was it Liz?"

"Yes, it was. But we're not married. Still together, living off-campus on Bryant Street. She has a job at the Gardner."

"So, you've overcome the pull of your genes?"

Adam cringed from Henry's assumption, hating the idea for, in his mind, he had always denied even the possibility.

"Look, Henry, there was no pull. What we did in that pool was, for me, exploration, pure and simple, and short-lived. I wish you'd do me a favor and just forget about it."

"Okay. Will do. But…"

"What were you saying?"

"Nothing. Except I'm glad you're here. That we're here together."

Adam thought he knew what Henry was about to say. His read on me is I'm fighting a pull, from whatever source God knows, but I'm fighting it, and someday, down the road, I'll have to own up to that fact. Sooner the better. He shook.

Henry caught the emotion Adam was experiencing. Obviously, the matter of sexual preference was off-limits. To change the subject, Henry asked how Liz found the Gardner.

"She likes the people more than the work, which is in restoration of old paintings. She's devoted to textiles. At the Gardner, the women outnumber the men. Liz finds that odd, given that the paintings they tend to are all by male artists."

"Nothing odd about it. The way of the world," Henry said.

The weeks of Adam's first year at law school seemed to fly by faster and faster, like pages turned by the reader of a riveting mystery impatient to get to its denouement. Liz and Adam settled into an SOS routine, their code for Sex Only Sunday. At first, Liz was astounded by her partner's work ethic. His powers of concentration seemed of a scale beyond human. In legal studies, she realized, he possessed a special intellectual acuity and discipline that seemed not to have surfaced before, in college, for example, where the results of his studies, while above the mean, were nothing special. He seemed driven by unseen forces to excel in the highly competitive setting of Harvard Law, where brilliance was commonplace, ambition to win almost universal and the largest factor in the race was the heights of preparedness and mastery to which motivation could carry one.

After a long Saturday in the library, they met on the stairs of Langdell and went to Hazen's for a simple dinner. "So, another day of toil for you, while I relaxed, shopped and read. What's driving you? It's as if you're in a sailing race in which life itself turns on crossing the finish line first."

"My goodness, you do have a way with words. Sailing's the perfect metaphor. One needn't pick a racing vessel. One can have all sorts of motor-driven boats. But if one had a racing vessel, wouldn't one want to enter races, and try to win? Entering Harvard Law, for me, was like buying a sleek racing yacht. Attending class, like raising the sails and heading for the starting line. I'm compelled to compete."

"And your father's role?" Liz smiled, licked her lips, then pursed them in suspicion.

"Yes, he dwells in my head. It's not a place to duck or hide."

"For better or worse?"

"Only time will tell."

Adam took his hasty lunches at Lincoln's Inn. He would occasionally bring Liz with him to the Inn for dinner, where they joined a number of law students to watch Huntley and Brinkley on TV describing 'contrapuntally', as the Tom Lehrer song put it, the dismal news dispatches of the day. Liz took note of the fact that on such occasions, she was the only female in attendance.

"Where are the women in this club? Surely, the gang that runs this law school knows it's not right to discriminate on the basis of gender." Liz put the question as they walked from the Inn to Bryant

Street. Her expression, highlighted by a street light, reflected a deliberate ambivalence between humor and shock.

"You know our class has only twenty or so women. The others even less. Not a large offering to pick from. But, surely you also know there's no discrimination. Not a chance. If women don't apply, it's hard to consider them."

Climbing the squeaky stairs to their apartment, Adam leading, the debate continued. "Okay. But, it sounds like an all-white jury considering the guilt of a Negro defendant."

"Liz, that analogy is absurd."

Catching her breath after following Adam through the door, she said, "Simply put, my point is that discrimination can be unconscious as well as conscious. Psych 101. If no one on that admissions committee can imagine women as members, they may achieve an unconscious yet deliberate goal of exclusion, even though the legal basis for it is missing. And word gets around. Women don't feel sought after by the elite law schools, to put it mildly."

Turning around to face her, he said, "I'm tired of arguing." He drew her close, wrapped his arms around her waist and said, "Let's plan our next trip to the movies."

❦

Liz was going to spend most of the summer with her parents, touring European cities, with a break from churches and art museums to spend a week hut hopping in the Stubai Alps of Austria. It was a trip promised long ago when she was a freshman in college but many times postponed due to conflicts her father developed in his post at DuPont.

Adam decided to take a job offer from a sole practitioner, arranged through this lawyer's son, Ben Solomon, a classmate of Adam's at Princeton. Working in a law firm after one's first year at law school was unusual. The opportunity just appeared, serendipitously, and he took it.

The bronze plaque on the door of the office at 14 Wall Street read "Abraham Solomon, Esquire." In addition to Mr. Solomon, there were three other lawyers. Adam would be the first, and only, summer associate. Ben assured Adam he had the job, and the interview his father requested was just a formality. "Of course, that's from Dad's perspective. From yours it could be different. You might not like him."

In the interview, Mr. Solomon asked Adam how he had done for the year.

"Well, the whole year turns on exams in June. Results not in. But I felt pretty good about how I handled them."

"Do you think you made the law review? You know, for us old-timers at the Law School, that's the Holy Grail."

"It's hard to know. Around the top 5% make it. That was my goal. I'd not be totally surprised if I got there."

"I like your attitude, Adam. For a lawyer, false modesty's not becoming."

Liz had left for Europe and Adam had started working for Mr. Solomon when he got a letter from Harvard, informing him that he ranked 12th out of 532 in his class, a pass to membership on the Harvard Law Review. Over dinner at home, he reported the news to his parents.

"Well, well, Adam, that's good news. You applied yourself and this splendid result followed. Quite a recovery from college results. Was it Liz who put your nose to the grindstone?" Wright smiled with obvious pleasure at his little joke.

Adam felt the warmth of his father's praise, which, despite his age, he sought like a hungry child in search of dinner.

"Actually, the reverse Father. She frequently called me driven. At times I felt that way."

Hannah said, "Something in the genes. From the male side."

⌘

Adam had Liz's itinerary. He wrote to her for delivery in Innsbruck.

July 8,1960

Dear Liz. This should reach you just before you embark on the hiking trip in the Stubai. Hope all is well. I am enjoying the work at Abraham Solomon. So different from law school, where one must deposit one's common sense in the Cambridge Bank. The work is practical, but creative and demanding in its practicality. Speaking of Harvard, I did well enough to make the Law Review. I think it was the sting of your whip that drove me there. If the year past was out of focus, the next one will be a total blur, given the demands of the Review. I hear that Gannett House is the home for many all-nighters. I just learned it was built in 1838!

You want to know how I feel about first year results? Well, the parents are pleased, so that's a big plus. You know Father was unhappy with my college results. He said more than once that he over-paid for small return. This compensates. Okay, I now hear you pressing me on how I really feel. You remember from *Guys and Dolls*, when Brando and Simmons return from PR, Simmons sings *If I were a Bell I'd be Ringing*? It's the song I've been singing in the showers since the results came in.

Take care, stay safe and have fun.

Love, Adam

Solomon's practice was unusually varied, from prize fighters to Madison Square Garden, from a European banking company to Jews seeking property stolen by the Nazis. And *Maxim's*, the world-famous Parisian restaurant then seeking to sell air-transported food in New York City. Of the three lawyers working for Mr. Solomon (partners or just employees Adam could never discern), he found himself working most frequently with Adrian Wu, a US-born Chinese-American whose parents landed as immigrants before he was born. Good with languages, Adrian spoke fluent French as well as impeccable English.

The four lawyers never went out for lunch. A good restaurant, just a block away, the kind with loud conversations, fast, brusque waiters, large portions and sawdust on the floor, was hired to cater lunches delivered to the firm's main conference room daily at 12:30. Adam felt lucky to be included in these luncheons, at which the topics for discussion included pending legal matters, but ranged across a much wider palette, the conference table becoming a canvas for discussion and debate on such matters as city politics, international affairs and sports—especially sports.

Adrian handled the *Maxim's* account. When a restaurant opened in Gramercy Park under the name *Maxim's,* using a logo and interior furnishings that were, in detail, identical to those used by the firm's Parisian client, Adrian brought Adam into deliberations over what to do. Adam researched the law involving "palming off," as it was known in commercial circles. They decided to seek a preliminary restraining order to stop the imposter from operating while the case continued. Adrian was confident the place would fold if that order could be obtained.

"So, Adam, we have the burden here. We must show a probability of winning the case in order to get the order. All we need is proof." Adrian smiled warmly, his smooth unwrinkled skin glowing. Adam liked working with Wu. And not only because he was very good at lawyering. Or because Adam was learning the trade almost every minute in Wu's presence.

Often, when Adam looked Adrian in the eye, he returned the look with what Adam believed was a hint of longing. It scared him. The exchange he thought dangerous. And, yet, he kept looking at Adrian, deliberately, irresistibly, invoking the same look back.

"What we need is the deposition of someone who has been to both restaurants. Someone who can validate with his eyes the claim of palming off. Any ideas?"

It was mid-August. Liz was arriving in a couple of days. Might she have been to *Maxim's* during her week in Paris? Given her parents' taste in restaurants, it wasn't out of the question.

❧

Adam was at the docks just before sundown to meet the Stuarts as they emerged from a first class cabin on the *SS Rotterdam*, Holland Lines' flagship. Passengers concentrated where the gangplank was to be lowered to the dock, looking like a massive jelly fish agitated and moving this way and that. The Stuarts pushed through the throng to reach Adam, with hugs and jolly greetings. The family would stay at the Waldorf for the night, then travel by train the next morning to home in Philadelphia.

Adam had never heard of the restaurant Henry Stuart had booked for dinner. Liz too was new to The Four Seasons and excited by the prospect. She had read somewhere that it was recently opened and swiftly had become an epicurean mecca defined by seasonally changing menus, American wines and wild mushrooms, among other unusual seasonal fare.

As they proceeded the short distance East from the hotel on 52nd, she said, "I'm looking forward to comparing The Four Seasons to the two star Michelin rated ones we dined at in Paris."

"Yes, good idea. Maybe *the Times* would be interested. I don't suppose one of them was *Maxim's*?"

"Didn't rate two stars, but we did dine there, mainly for the atmosphere. Food was so-so."

"Wow! What luck! Have I got a job for you. Let's talk later."

They were seated in the Pool Room. The pretensions of the place filled Adam's nostrils. Located in the famously bronze Seagram's Headquarters on Park Avenue, close to the Waldorf on 52nd Street, it had been designed by Mies van der Rohe and Philip Johnson, the architects who were responsible for the building itself. The interior was filled with distinguished art, including a large hanging curtain by Pablo Picasso. And the stunning serviceware had been designed by L. Garth and Ada Louise Huxtable.

Henry ordered a California red wine for the table, smelling the cork handed to him by the Sommelier in that ancient, well-honed practice. Inhaling deeply, he nodded approval. "I think this should meet our needs," Henry said, as the Sommelier emptied the well-aged wine into an eloquently shaped decanter, deep red sparkling through crystal.

As they walked back to the Waldorf, Henry said he thought The Four Seasons lived up to its reputation. "And even its pretensions," Liz added, laughing over a tummy filled close to the brim.

Adam had warmed to those pretensions. He imagined how much his father would have enjoyed the evening. Although they might not admit it, the scene at The Four Seasons, with its trappings of high style and insouciant wealth, was one both father and son coveted.

Liz met Adam outside *Maxim's* on 20th Street and Gramercy Park. Primed to take note of each and every detail, the décor, the menu, the tables and chairs, Liz first brought forth from her memory bank the images of the Parisian *Maxim's*, then made a mental palimpsest of all around her.

Once in the restaurant, Liz was bubbling over with the thrill of realizing how useful she was going to be. Breathless, she whispered across the table.

"What did you call it? 'Palming off.' Well, they did it with the mirrors, the murals of nymphs, the stained glass ceiling, the Art Nouveau lamps. These can't be accidents. I could go on. The red and white menus, the red and gold awnings outside. I tell you, Adam, it palming off down to the last detail."

Adam contained his own excitement, which grew with each whispered act of deliberate imitation.

Adam said "We've got more than enough. Let's just order a bowl of soup and get out of here."

"Wait, Adam. I want to do a bit of fishing."

The waiter arrived. They ordered vichyssoise and French bread, announcing they were too pressed for time to have more.

"I've just returned from Paris, where I had a fine meal at the *Maxim's* there. Your décor is so much the same that I wonder, are you under common ownership with the French restaurant?"

"No connection. Except the décor. As you note, we copied them down to the last detail. Pretty nice, huh?"

"Indeed!" replied Liz, almost undone at the success of her troll, a look of shocked delight breaking out across her face.

Later, under oath, she was deposed by her lover, who, naturally enough, omitted that detail in identifying himself to the transcriptionist. In the deposition, Liz was able to identify all the concrete acts of palming off, ending with the waiter's unknowing strike at her lure. A Temporary Restraining Order was issued against continued operations until the case was concluded. With that the imposter closed its doors for good.

Abraham Solomon was delighted. To celebrate, he took Adrian and Adam to a fancy luncheon on the wharf at the foot of Wall Street, where they sampled oysters on the half shell and lobster rolls good enough to rival the best in Maine. Abe, as he insisted on being called, was forthright in urging Adam to return the following summer and then accept a permanent position with the firm.

"Don't answer now. I'll be frank. You're good. You have high potential. We'd like that potential to be realized in our firm. Let the offer sink in. It won't be withdrawn."

That night Adam had a dream. A bedroom scene with Adrian removing his last piece of clothing. Alarmed, he instructed himself not to take the incident seriously. Dreams are just fantasies triggered by smells or a dog's bark, a car's horn or whatever. His dream signified nothing. Instead, he forced himself to recall Liz's brilliance in the deposition.

One day in the spring of Adam's second year, Hector Humphrey, a classmate whom Adam knew well from his singing days with the Nassoons, invited him to become a member of the Choate Club, an institution he had never heard of. His friend explained the club was a tightly held secret, known only to its members, who included both students and faculty. It had been around for decades, serving simply the purpose of assembling a group of convivial members around a dinner table at the Signet Society for good food, drink and serious conversation, usually focused on a subject presented by a dinner speaker. Considering it an honor to be asked, Adam joined. He decided not to tell Liz, knowing she'd attack him for entering another elite group lacking female members, which he assumed safely to be the case. But when it came time for him to attend his first Choate dinner, he chose not to lie about where he was going, especially as it necessitated rescheduling a dinner with friends that Liz was in the process of planning for the same night.

"Tell me about this club."

"I will be late if I don't go now. Talk later." He vanished down the steps, sounding to her like an escaping scoundrel.

Adam's first encounter with the Choate Club exposed him to a self-selected group of students, pollinated by a number of faculty, all of whom, like the faculty in general, had enlarged intellectual pretensions that could not easily be dismissed, because they were, for the most part, justified. But, still, the experience was too enjoyable, too exclusive, too self-satisfied, to be, for Adam, just put away in his memory without some concern and examination. Indeed, in worrying about joining such an exclusive and secret institution, he had the added burden of being periodically reminded of Liz's disapproval. Despite her upper-class trappings and a history of being placed by her parents in elite institutions as well as in Philadelphia's Social Register, by dint of which she was expected to come out as a debutante and, in fact, did so in order to avoid a fight with her parents, she was an egalitarian, through and through. In fact, she often thought these trappings of wealth and status could be blamed for turning her around, accounting for her leveling perspective on life.

The speaker at that first dinner was R. Sargent Shriver, brother-in-law to Jack Kennedy, recently elected President. Shriver spoke about the Peace Corps, created by the President in an Executive Order only a few weeks before the Choate Club members sat down to dinner. He had been appointed the Corps' first Director in early March of '61.

It was distinctly a coup to have him speak. All thanks to Professor Paul Bator, a member of the Choate who had arranged the event. Shriver described the accidental talk Kennedy gave in Ann Arbor as a creative, spur-of-the-moment invention of the then candidate as he fought sleep to speak to an audience of some 10,000 waiting at the Michigan Union at 2 in the morning, the time of his delayed arrival in this university town. Speaking from the heart rather than the head, he asked the crowd something to this effect: "How many of you would be willing to serve this country and the cause of peace by living and working in the developing world?" The response in following days was overwhelming. The Executive Order followed, creating the Peace Corps. Training for work in Tanganyika, Columbia and Ghana began soon after and was then underway. We expect, Shriver proudly announced, the first contingent of teachers to land in Accra by August.

What dazzled Adam and others around the table at the Signet was a powerful sense of youthful support and energy for the Peace Corps. And the serendipity of the spark that brought it to life: an inadvertent sentence uttered by an exhausted campaigner set down past midnight in Ann Arbor and desperate for sleep. Shriver suggested that, while ambition drove him to speak to the gathering, it was heart-felt inspiration that formed his words and the creative idea they expressed. For Adam, it was a brilliant beginning for his Choate Club membership. Even Liz, after overcoming her outrage at Adam's involvement with what she called "an exclusive, secret society for boys only, playing men," grudgingly admitted to being impressed.

"I wish I had been there," she said, a challenging smile lining her face.

❧ 10 ❧

1961-1962

"Adam, you've made us proud."

It was spring of 1961. It had been an all-consuming year on the Law Review for Adam, with his studies being dragged along, like a prisoner roped behind a horse and rider. Liz saw very little of him as the months raced by.

Wright was at his desk in his home office and Adam, home for a quick Easter visit, was sitting opposite, feeling, for once, taller than his father, despite the reality of Wright's pre-adjusted chair. Adam had just reported on his election by his colleagues to be Editor-in-Chief.

"It doesn't get much better than that," Wright exclaimed. "Now, the next step is a clerkship. Given your position at the Review, I see no reason why you shouldn't be able to have your pick of justices."

Adam had expected his father to move swiftly up to the next rung on his son's ladder, one in Dwight's mind stretching into the clouds. Expected and depressing.

"The election gives me a leg up, that's for sure, but you've always taught me not to count the chicken before it hatches. All we've got here is an egg. Would you have a preference?"

"Look, you're dealing with the Warren court. Too liberal for my taste. Potter Stewart is a moderate, far to the right of Warren and his acolytes. And he's pragmatic. He should be your choice."

Adam winced. He stared at the wart on his father's left cheek, imagining that it had reddened. He regretted having raised the question.

"Father, the reasons Stewart appeals to you are exactly the ones that hold no appeal for me. I'd like to try for Brennan. I admire his expansive view of the First Amendment. His opposition to the death penalty. And his support for abortion rights."

Wright recoiled in surprise, shocked by Adam's blunt disagreement.

"Well, I don't welcome your reasoning. Not a bit. But, far be it from me to insist. You've earned the right to choose. I'm only urging—and do so only because of my long experience with the Court—yes, and my exposure to these Constitutional issues—I'm urging you, as your father, but also as a law professor, to go after Potter Stewart. To put it plainly, clerk for Brennan and his reputation rubs off on you. That could hurt down the road. In fact, you might be taken for a Communist."

As Editor-in-Chief of the Harvard Law Review, not getting a Supreme Court appointment would be surprising, and equally so not accepting one if offered. But the process was anything but straight-forward. Adam resented his father opening the subject up before Adam had even assumed the duties of Editor-in-Chief. And was disappointed in himself for engaging.

The mystery of clerkship selection resided in the sorting process the Harvard Professors did among themselves, ending up with offers to the top students to write on their behalf to particular Justices with whom they had close connections, whether through having been clerks themselves or in other ways. Thus it was, in December, that the Potter Stewart Committee of Harvard Professors, consisting of Archibald Cox and Paul Freund, offered to recommend Adam for a Stewart clerkship. Adam had let the Committee know of his interest, having decided, reluctantly and with growing anger at the enormous pressure that continued from his father, despite his promise to back off, to try for a Stewart post.

He felt better about the decision when Professor Cox told him, *sotto voce,* that, given the attraction of Justice Brennan among students at Harvard, Yale and Columbia, his chances with that Justice were slimmer than with Stewart. And, Cox added that, in his opinion, Justice Stewart was moving steadily to the left of the position he occupied on the Circuit Court, and, therefore, moving him further in that direction was a feasible goal for a clerk, and a worthy one for Adam to undertake. Brennan, on the other hand, was rooted on the left, leaving little for his clerks to do other than express his settled interpretations of the Constitution in draft memoranda and opinions. Finally, Cox said, with deliberately modest mien, the Committee's reputation with the Justice was such that, barring a disastrous interview, the post should be his.

Adam was accepted for a clerkship with Justice Stewart, beginning in the summer of 1962.

As his days as a third-year student passed, Adam felt growing pressure to marry Liz. It came from his parents, from Liz and even occasionally from her parents. With thematic variations, the cry was "Enough Already." In his mind marriage gradually emerged as the single easiest way to make all those around him happy. Next to producing a healthy baby, the best. He recognized, in quiet moments of loneliness, the ambiguity of his sexuality. From whatever source or sources it came, and he had no clue to lead him to the answer, it was a fact of his life, a fact that could not be ducked, forgotten or erased. Like an engagement ring that, with age and an arthritic finger, could no longer be taken off, it stalked his mind, restraining him with uncertainty about whether marriage to Liz, or for that matter to any woman, was for him the right step to take. At least until his sexual identity could come more sharply into focus. But, he discovered, the pesky problem was simply that the focus needed couldn't just be summoned, and the shadow of his father weighed heavily in the mix.

Adam knew anything other than marriage, indeed, in Father's terms, a "proper marriage," would not do for the Hudson family. And, finally, to muddle his mind even more, he feared that marriage would not, indeed, could not, down the road, prevent his discovery of a preference for men, if such was in fact the truth. Hadn't Henry Wolfson warned him about the 'pull' of his genes, a warning given when they first met as first year law students, one that he could neither forget nor address. Seeing risks everywhere, he finally came to believe marriage the least difficult course to follow. Although he also feared it might harbor seeds for painful outcomes in the future. And he wondered if he was being honest with himself. But at the end of the day, his analysis led to one final and compelling idea, rooted in the optimism with which he was born. Why he asked himself couldn't the very ambiguity of his sexuality mean he could enjoy a happy and fulfilling life either straight or gay? All he had to do was come down definitely on one side or the other. Marriage, he concluded, would be the answer, the glue to hold firm the decision.

They married in late October, 1962, following graduation and the start of Adam's clerkship. The Hudsons followed custom in hosting a bridal dinner the night before the wedding, a relatively small affair involving only the families of bride and groom, the bridesmaids and Adam's ushers. It was held at the Franklin Inn Club, which offered reciprocal privileges to members of the University Club in New York City, a club to which Wright Hudson belonged. The dinner was a triumph of Hannah's exquisite planning and execution. The wedding occurred at St. Paul's Episcopal Church on East Chestnut Hill Avenue, the church attended by the Stuart family, and the reception was hosted by the Stuarts under a white tent erected in the ample grassy yard of their home in Bala Cynwyd.

St. Paul's was high Episcopal, identical in most respects to Anglican in the United Kingdom. In the rehearsal for the wedding, held the morning before the wedding day, Adam and Liz were joined by both sets of parents, eager to soak up every aspect of this time-honored program, one that could be conducted simply in Quaker style befitting a Philadelphia locus, or with varying levels of ceremony and pomp offered by the Episcopal Church. Both sets of parents, resisting protestations from the leading actors in the performance, had insisted on the highest levels offered at St. Paul's.

The rehearsal proceeded smoothly until the vows. Taken from the *Book of Common Prayer*, they differed in only one respect. The groom says "to love and to cherish till death do us part" while the bride says "to love, to cherish and to obey till death do us part."

Liz balked at promising to obey Adam. "I can't pledge such a thing. I'd be lying if I did, and I'm sure the higher powers at St. Paul's would know it, and take steps."

Adam said, "I would never ask for obedience, or expect it. Just drop those words and make the two pledges the same."

Wright said, "There's no choice in the matter. If it's in the Good Book, it can't be changed."

The Stuarts nodded in agreement, turning Liz red with rage.

"You won't impose this verb on me. Every scrap of the education you insisted I absorb wars against the idea. If necessary, we will find a Justice of the Peace. "

Hoping to resolve the impasse, the priest said, simply, "We can delete those words. It's been done many times, especially in recent years."

Hannah had been alarmed to the point of shock by what appeared to be an insurmountable conflict. Knowing Wright, she knew he was unlikely to yield easily on a matter of principle, especially when enshrined in Christian history. And so, when the Priest offered a solution, she jumped on it.

"Problem solved! Thank you Reverend Kinsolving."

If Hannah had looked at her husband, she would have seen a face turned scarlet with anger, his ears smoking, yes, and even more so at the frustration of having been silenced so deftly by his wife.

Throughout this bump in the road to marriage, Adam was deep in thought. He contrasted the ease of solving the issue of their vows with the stroke of a pen to the insanely difficult problem of solving his sexuality. Wright often reduced family problems to that simplistic 'Hope for the best; plan for the worst.' Adam did not see how his problem could be solved with that formula. He was entering matrimony with hope but no plan for failure, having imposed on himself the idea that marriage was the way to escape the uncertainty that had plagued him since childhood.

Wright Hudson was Adam's "best man," selected by what Wright described as a family decision, where a majority ruled, where Hannah was lashed to her husband's mast and where any disagreement by Adam could be out-voted by his parents. So often in Adam's teenage years, and through college and law school, this process had been used by his father to assert himself through the façade of family democracy. Adam now, as so often on past occasions, was tempted to ridicule it. But the memory of painful incidents over the years blocked a turn to humor.

Adam had four ushers in addition to his father, including Henry Wolfson, Hector Humphrey, and two others drawn from the ranks of his closest friends at Cap and Gown. They threw a bachelor's party for Adam two nights before the wedding, held, like the Bridal Dinner the next evening, at the Franklin Inn Club. Adam was hoping to discourage his father from attending, although he knew an invitation had to be made. He was sure Wright's presence would change the tenor of the evening, and not for the better. He knew as well that his ushers would be pleased if, somehow, Adam could bring his father to the point of declining the honor of being present.

No dice. Wright insisted on attending. He seemed to fill the room, dominating the conversation, listening to the others hardly at all, and creating a dour and repressed feeling around the room. It proved to be a clash not only of generations but of personalities, leaving a foul taste in the mouths of all save Wright, who, tone-deaf to all around him, when the party was over, declared it an especially enjoyable evening.

At the bridal dinner the following night, there were many speeches, some long, some short, some funny, some wanting in purpose or wit. As host, best man and father to the groom, Wright Hudson achieved a kind of hat-trick. He spoke early in the evening, before drinks and wine had dulled the collective senses.

"This wedding is a big occasion for Hannah and me. We only have one off-spring, a fact that concentrates the mind when parents are faced with giving that one and only away in marriage.

We face this task with happiness. In picking Liz Stuart, we think Adam has made the right choice, one we couldn't be more pleased about. In truth, we have been awaiting this moment for some time. Adam was a late bloomer in respect to the opposite sex, as he was in academics and athletics. When he was a teenager we had the common problem of deciding how his character should be developed. He needed to be taught how to carry through on a tedious task over a long period of time. We used many approaches, including piano lessons, dancing lessons, singing lessons—you name it and we could probably say we tried it. Despite all this, Adam made better friends than he did grades in high school and college. But when he entered law school, his alarm clock went off. He began to fulfill the potential we saw in him. And what followed was the Law Review and, ultimately, election to the Presidency of that distinguished body. And then by a Supreme Court clerkship. Our molding was complete. And now, here's the icing on the cake, if you will, Adam's forthcoming marriage to Liz. We are so proud. Please join me in raising a glass to them both, wishing long life and fulfilling purpose."

The evening wound down and guests turned homeward, leaving members of the Hudson family happy with the way they played their parts.

To Adam and Liz, the wedding and reception were a blur, with time racing around a clock gone haywire until at last they drove off amidst the usual cheers and throwing of rice. Families of bride and groom, together with the closest of friends, made for a small gathering of less than one hundred, but no less enthusiastic on that account.

The newly married couple were headed north, first for the night in Princeton, staying at the Nassau Inn, scene of their first breakfast together, and then on to New York City, where they had a summer sublease enabling Adam to study for the New York bar exam.

Adam's law school friends, Henry Wolfson and Hector Humphrey, were at the reception. So, too, were Abraham Solomon and Adrian Wu. These four, knowing Adam well, but in different ways, found pleasure in sharing a common admiration for their friend, a process that consumed time enough for a couple of glasses of champagne.

"Adam's a man of many parts," Abe said. "In his work with us last summer, he developed a reputation for never wanting to be put a question for which he lacked an answer. He seemed embarrassed, almost humiliated, when that rare event happened. Once, I asked him about it and he acknowledged the issue. I advised him to get over it, because the practice of law involves a constant stream of questions from clients for which the lawyer has no answer. That's the secret glory of the practice. Can you imagine being paid a fee to find the answer to a client's question?"

"And did he take your advice to heart?" Hector asked.

"Perhaps. To heart, likely. To head, who knows. The summer was too short to discover."

Henry said "Adam was on his game today. As if he'd rehearsed the whole thing many times. Performed beautifully throughout."

Adrian joined the conversation. "I bet it was carefully rehearsed. Last summer I worked with Adam over many hours and on many different matters. He was a determined man, if not driven, in hating to waste time, in being plu-perfectly prepared, in never wanting to be caught unaware. I thought his identity centered on being a lawyer, until I learned of his mastery of sailing and singing. And limericks, for goodness sakes. He's a proud man. Liz will have her hands full keeping up with him."

Henry noticed Adam untangled by admirers and moved to speak with him.

"You're a groom to admire, Adam. Had a brief talk with Liz. She's terrific. I'm so happy for you both. You want to know something funny? I was going to suggest you list in the Princeton Gay Alumni Directory. That was before I learned you were getting married."

"Henry, please. This is not the time or place. Ancient history."

"You're right. Stupid me. I'm sorry."

Adam saw Henry as a genie who appeared at his ear when least welcome, whispering reminders of a past laden with the ambiguities he was trying to leave behind.

❧ 11 ❧

1962-1964

It had been a hectic summer, the marriage, then the sublease in New York City, studying for the Bar Exam and sitting for it at the end of August, then moving to DC where they found another apartment, fully furnished and available due to its owner, a State Department Officer, having been suddenly posted to Ghana. He even left them his car, a vintage Pontiac. And, following all these preparations, the clerkship with Justice Potter Stewart.

Adam had long known he would return to the Metropolitan area and join a NYC law firm. He picked Bundy, Rogers and Freund for no better reason than praise from his boss, Potter Stewart, who knew the firm, had interviewed for a summer job there during his second year at law school and, he humorously allowed, had been forgotten when the firm accidently lost the record of his having interviewed on campus and, therefore, never scheduled interviews at the firm. In mid-summer, Phillip Rogers, the partner who interviewed him at law school, wrote a graceful apology to Stewart, who had taken a summer job at Cleary, Gottlieb. Remarkably, the future Justice never held the experience against Bundy; indeed, his admiration grew with time and with it the humor he found in this little screw-up. Over the year of clerking, Adam came to know Potter Stewart well, which meant admiring his enduring capacity to put himself in the other's shoes before judging, as he did with the Bundy firm, in understanding the institutional pain and embarrassment of the mistake that lost a promising applicant's resume.

Before accepting the Bundy firm offer, Adam did more homework than just taking the Justice's word for it. He called Timothy Bright, a Stewart clerk who had gone to Bundy in 1959. Bright gave the firm high marks, expressed pleasure in being there, especially given the humanity of the place and its professional integrity, and the deeply held notion that all clients are firm clients, regardless of who attracted them or does their work. He said he came to Bundy principally on the Justice's recommendation. As to how it compared to being a Stewart clerk, he simply replied: "A letdown."

In an odd way, Timothy's candor impressed Adam. After all, any Supreme Court clerk, going to a NYC law firm, would likely experience a letdown. Admitting it, however, to one who must have been viewed by Timothy a prize catch would seem a confession against interest, and therefore curious. Adam thought it worthy. He thought the firm sounded like a community instead of a bunch of desks occupied by lawyers out for themselves. Transferring Timothy's worthiness more generally to Bundy, Rogers and Freund, he picked up the offer.

Adam's period of apprenticeship at Bundy was short. His first annual review was delivered by Jim Bundy in the senior partner's generous office, a space Adam had never visited until summoned for the review by Mildred White, Bundy's hawk-eyed secretary, who had served him with loyalty and growing skill for more than two decades. Until recently, he had been the operations head of the firm, but had turned that big but unappreciated job over to George Banville.

The senior partner invited Adam to sit in a comfortable chair beside a coffee table, then came around his desk to sit in another chair near the table. Adam noted with a wry smile the absence of any height difference.

"Well, Adam, one year under your belt. How did it feel?"

"It's been a good year, sir. No shortage of work. I took the good advice Mr. Rogers gave me at the start, not to take on too much, try my best with each assignment and measure the results against the standards expected by the firm."

"Sound advice. I wish more of our young associates would accept that idea. How do you think the quality of your work ranked against our standards?"

Miss White had appeared muscling a heavy tray with a pot of coffee, cups, cream and sugar which she slid gracefully onto the table.

"Let's have some coffee, before you answer that." Bundy poured two cups.

"I thought that's what I'm here to find out. But if you like, I'll try to reckon it."

"I have a better idea. Don't answer that. Quite right. Silly to have asked you. Not here for a self-evaluation. Not a bit. Let me tell you what we think of your first year." Bundy's smile and manner put Adam at ease.

Adam nodded. "Okay." He hadn't been eager to answer the question, one likely to get him into trouble no matter how he responded.

"Your written work has been, from the outset, marked by economy, precision, and accuracy. Some for whom you worked mentioned that these qualities were often wrapped in an elegant style. One partner, after observing you on several matters, suggested that the hurdle you set for yourself was a level of excellence one notch higher than the level you had just attained. You've earned unvarying praise, uniform marks of distinction in a challenging environment. With our congratulations comes a raise of $5,000, meaning your salary beginning today will be at the annual rate of $14,000."

"Thank you, sir. As I said, I felt it had been a good year. Your review confirms it."

"Indeed. To put a point on Jim Rogers' advice, our consensus is that you noticeably exceeded the firm's standards of excellence. Now, all you need to do in the coming year is drag the rest of the firm along." Bundy's face broke out in a mischievous smile, followed by a laugh that seemed to shake his small frame, top to bottom. Adam hoped his boss had been joking.

Leaning forward, speaking in undertones, Bundy said, "Where, may I ask, Adam, did you acquire your standards of excellence?"

"It was easy. By inheritance." Adam saw Jim Bundy as sort of a father-figure, at least within the firm's community, one who carried the firm's values on his shoulders, one it was easy to open up to.

"I must have internalized my parents' standards. It seemed, growing up, that they never could be truly satisfied with the quality of my work. As a result, I couldn't be satisfied either. They seemed to expect perfection. Of course I always fell short. Coming back to your review, sir, isn't there something in the record suggesting possible improvement?"

Bundy flipped through the pages of his summary.

"Oh, here's a point. A small one but I should have mentioned it. On one occasion you apparently reached a legal conclusion based on facts that in one respect you got wrong. The correct facts wouldn't have changed your conclusion, which was correct. But it could have been different. The facts come first and must be mastered. Here's a story you might enjoy. About Arturo Toscanini. Just moments before the performance of a long and complex symphony, one of the woodwind players discovered that his B flat key was broken. In a panic the musician rushed to Toscanini and asked that the performance be delayed. Toscanini paused for a brief moment and then said, 'Don't worry—there's no B flat note for you to play in tonight's program.'"

Thrilled by his review, Adam left Bundy's office with a bounce to his step.

⟐

For his first two years at the firm, Adam shared an office with Andrew Jenkins, who had transferred to Bundy after two years of thankless hours tallied up as an associate with Cravath, where he had spent himself in the dark realms of discovery in the mammoth antitrust case brought by the Justice Department against Cravath's client, IBM.

Swiftly, Adam and Andy became close friends. They often found themselves working through the evening and shared an attitude that said, 'get the work done, whatever it takes, then a drink and modest dinner (lest they won't sleep), then home to bed.' This custom, as it evolved, often kept them at work until about nine, when they would depart for the Brasserie, a French bistro in the basement of the Seagram's building. They would sit at the bar, tease the waitress, who came to know them, and order double martinis on the rocks, lemon twist for Adam, pearly onions for Andy. Then French onion soup for both, followed by such things as mushroom omelet, fromage-burger or Caesar salad.

Often they were too tired to talk about anything serious. But one night, they got started on the subject of fathers, after Andy mentioned that his father had died unexpectedly during the War, when Andy was nine, due to a hospital infection.

"Yeah, no penicillin in the hospitals in '44. What there was had been shipped to the front lines. Great for the troops. But not for my dad. A simple colon fix led to death from an infection that could easily have been wiped out by penicillin. A sad matter of timing. I assume your dad is still around?"

Adam was just finishing off the onion soup. He tried to fit into Andy's shoes, to imagine the pain of a nine-year old told his father was dead. The shoes didn't fit. He turned to Andy's question, looking around the near empty restaurant to be sure no one was within earshot.

"He's very definitely still around. It's hard—no, impossible—to imagine him not being here, hovering just above my head, watching every move I make. I've never imagined life without him."

The fromage-burgers, perfectly pink and surrounded with cornichons, purple onion and French fries, had been put down in front of them, following removal of the soup bowls.

"So, you'd miss him? His influence on you, I gather, has been large. I think you told me you were an only child."

"Yeah."

Adam felt the effects of the double martini. Like a truth serum, it loosened the tongue, which was okay; he welcomed the chance to undress.

"Growing up, I loved having him take charge. In a way, I guess, it became an excuse for not making decisions myself. The headwinds to resistance were strong. And so, here I sit, having gone to the college of his choice, the law school of his choice, the clerkship of his choice, and married the wife of his choice. And many other things. The fact that he was often right didn't make things easier or lessen the resentment when I caved, as I did most of the time. Often, growing up, I felt like a trained seal. I'm sure he actually thought of himself as the trainer. I saw no way to escape his influence. It persists today, and that's the bitter part. I never figured out a way to resist without breaking the bond, and that's the only choice he offered. I suppose I was weak. It's my little failure." Adam pursed his lips, then sucked the lower one in against his teeth. "So, what about you?"

"Hey, that's quite a mouthful. Let's see. Memory of my dad is diluted, although I could as easily say enriched, by the memories of so many of his close friends, who often told me their stories about him. Within five years of his death, my own memory was—how to put it—infiltrated by the memories of others. It got to the point where the two strands of truth were woven together. I couldn't separate them. From then on he became a sort of legend, a very good one, but not useful in the decisions I had to make, day to day."

Adam tried to imagine his home without Father. Thought turned to fog. He looked at Andy, sadness writ large across his face. "It's hard to fathom losing a father at nine."

"Here's the surprising thing. As the years passed, I found I could collect fathers. Lacking the one enabled the collection of many. I could identify with those within my circle who offered me guidance. You know, modeling of one kind or another. And, when I had squeezed all the fatherly value from one surrogate, I could move on, perhaps to another surrogate. The key was the freedom to move on, to pick and choose, to latch on to someone willing to be a mentor. For you, I imagine, this freedom was not available."

"Ouch! Andy, you *do* have a way to pinpoint an issue. Must be the secret to your success as a lawyer. The fact is I have one father, and for better or worse, he's there for me, whether, in growing up, I wanted him there quite so much or not. My son, George, is in a Montessori pre-school on the Upper West Side. I'm very involved with the school and what I've noticed is the indulgence, care and attention given to the first born by parents with kids in the school. It's taken to extremes, which seem to vanish with the second and even more with the third. I think this phenomenon is universal and explains the extreme degree to which my father undertook the task of molding me, an only child, in his …….. to his liking."

"You almost said 'in his image'."

"Perhaps that was his goal. I don't know. If challenged, I do know he'd deny it. How different would I be if I'd grown up from nine without a father? Or you, if you'd had one? I suppose this is just part of the nurture/nature debate. But I know there are parts of me that are very much like my father, and mostly they are parts I don't like but can't seem to shake."

"At the end of the day, that debate is unresolved, the answers unknowable. There's one thing I do know. It's time to pay up and wend our way home."

Adam quickly changed from student to teacher at Bundy, where his reputation spread among younger associates, who enjoyed sitting at his feet. He became known for an obsession with the perfectly drafted clause, comparing the drafting of contracts with the building of a wooden boat by hand, a process, he pronounced, requiring drafting skill, yes, but beyond that, the elements of loving care. Unfortunately, this attention to detail sometimes came across as excessive, a personal indulgence that served his own value system more than those of the younger associates working with him, or for that matter the clients. Here was an impact within the firm, among his colleagues, that he missed understanding, despite his generally well developed skill at reading the reactions of clients and others outside the firm.

In the course of his second review, after two years at the firm, Jim Bundy, reviewing his 2900 billable hours, a peak among associates and far above the expected level, asked Adam to explain what he called "an excessive number of hours."

"I don't know what to say. The work is intellectually interesting. I even find it relaxing at times. You know, the comradeship and all. More so than other things I might do. It's not a problem is it? Let me add, I'm not driven to put in so much time because of worry over how I'm viewed by the firm. Not at all. I feel valued, with a future here."

Bundy got up from his desk and walked to the window, staring down Park Avenue. Turning to face Adam, he said, "This is not a problem for the firm. We know your reputation as a perfectionist. But also for being devilishly efficient. So clients are not suffering. And, obviously we benefit on the back of your labor. But there's Liz and George. More hours here mean less hours with them. And your other interests, like sailing and singing. Or involving yourself in City Bar Association work or other civic affairs. We try to concern ourselves with the whole lives of our lawyers, with the potential for a full career with us, and to be there for them when needed. In your case, the hours seem excessive, and that's a worry. Are you leaving time for other things?"

"That's a question I've asked myself. And one Liz has put to me. And the answer is, I just don't know. Working elbow to elbow with younger associates is a solid satisfaction; they're so eager, like dry sponges soaking up all I have to offer. But beyond that it just seems I belong here, working, as long as there is work to do."

Bundy returned to his desk. His face took on the look of a caring parent.

"May I ask a personal question?" Adam nodded.

"Have you ever considered your huge hours here an escape strategy?"

"Oh, no sir. I don't know anything I need to escape from."

"Okay, I'm just going to ask you to keep an eye on your hours. You're too valuable to the firm, and, of course, to your family and yourself, to run the risk of a burnout from over-work."

After his meeting with Bundy, Adam began more seriously to ponder his hours, to see them as an outcropping, revealing of things covered over. Bundy's question about escape got to him. He'd never considered the totality of his work, measured in hours. He knew he worked hard, but he didn't know his hours so far exceeded those of others, or were so far above the firm's expectations, which had never been spelled out. The idea that work with colleagues, elbow to elbow, was a release or escape from something hit him hard, becoming more than a possibility, as he weighed it, but what that 'something' was he lacked the insight to find, or possibly the will to find, fearing the consequences.

1970-1985

Adam became a partner in Bundy, Adams and Freund in the record time of six years, as did Andy. Normal seasoning took eight. Adam was in the same law school class as his colleague and friend, Richard Halpert, who had ripened rapidly into a valuable tax lawyer. In fact, invaluable. When he informed the firm that he had been offered a partnership in a DC firm specializing in tax matters and was more than slightly tempted, the Bundy firm decided to make him a partner forthwith, along with the two other partner-track associates from the same class. As the story circulated among the associates, Jim Bundy was heard to explain: "Bundy's set in its ways, fiercely proud and often inflexible, but not proud and inflexible to the point of stupidity, not at the cost of losing the young tax genius they had carefully molded for their own purposes."

Partners were given annual reviews. Jim Bundy continued his pleasant chore of reviewing Adam. All was positive except for the hours, which continued to increase, year to year after partnership, growing to an astounding 3200 in 1979. Adam sat in front of Jim Bundy's imposing desk, a large turn of the century monster, made of black walnut with carved edges of graceful laurel. It radiated probity, ancient tradition, long-lasting power and intellectual heft.

"Your hours continue to increase. They're way too high. Well above the Plimsoll Line for this firm. And above the level of health for you and your family. What are we to do? You're a recidivist. Yours is a problem we've never had to cope with before. All our firm's policies are designed with the goal of growing billable hours, and income. We never had need for the reverse. You are known to have solutions for everything. What's the solution here?" Bundy's voice had the ring of command.

"Well, we've talked about this before. I'm no wiser as to what's behind the long hours—if anything. They seem to fly by. I enjoy the teaching part of this work more than just the work itself, or the satisfaction of collecting a bill and being thanked by the client. Much more. Since there's always more work, and more one can teach, I guess that's the best explanation I can come up with."

"Someone wiser in the ways of mankind might say, as I suggested to you before, that you're trying to escape from something."

Adam responded swiftly, emphatically, as if he were trying to convince not only Jim Bundy.

"Not a chance. With all respect, I don't accept that idea."

Adam took on a client from Columbus, Ohio, Jane Howland, a widow with one college-age son, who owned a large share of a newspaper, radio and TV business long controlled and operated by other members of the extended Howland family. Turmoil within the family over how the business was being conducted brought the contesting members to cash out by auctioning off the business in its severable parts. Morgan Stanley was retained to conduct the auction. The Bundy firm was retained through Adam, who knew Jane Howland, to represent her family's interests in the separate auctions of the newspaper and the radio/tv stations. Adam felt fortunate in getting Eric Slattery, a young associate of wit, brains and high promise, to work with him on this project. He had been an editor of the Yale Daily News and loved journalism. The Howland corporations had their own counsel, who was expected to take the lead in document preparation and such limited negotiation as might be necessary with the successful bidders. Jane Howland wanted Adam to oversee the Ohio firm's work and participate in the drafting and negotiations to the extent he thought useful to protect Jane's interests.

The sale documents for the two auctioned properties were, to Adam and Eric's eyes, poorly drafted for the purposes intended. They set to work perfecting them in the manner customary for the Bundy firm, which called for them to imagine and address every conceivable risk. It took time and the client's money. As one frustrated client was heard to remark, "There's harmony of purpose for them in being so extraordinarily risk-averse and detail oriented, and in the fattened bottom line this approach to lawyering yields."

Within this circle of firm-wide enhanced care, Adam's renown as a perfectionist shone brighter than any. And he relished this reputation.

The sales were based on, among other factors, the audited financials, going back five years. Montgomery, the local accounting firm in Columbus, had been used by the Howland businesses for more than a decade. They affirmed to the Howlands, who in turn affirmed in the sale documents to the buyers, that the five year financials were correct and had been prepared in accordance with generally accepted accounting principles. There were many representations and warranties made by the Howlands in the sale documents, but none were as important to the buyers as those vouching for the financials.

The newspaper was sold without a hitch. The sale of the radio/tv stations, however, was marred by the buyer's discovery, after the sale was completed, of accounting errors in the financials on which the buyer had relied. The buyer sued to rescind the transaction and won. The Howlands turned to the Montgomery firm to recover its loss, its error being indisputably negligent. Given the careful drafting signed off on by Adam and Eric, Montgomery was clearly liable to the Howlands. But there was a problem. The sale price was $100 million. Montgomery was a small firm with no hard assets and only $500,000 of professional insurance coverage. Despite the care lavished on the sale documents by both the Ohio firm and Adam and Eric, no one had thought to ask about insurance or what other source Montgomery might have to cover a loss arising from negligent auditing errors. And yet, as all parties to the transaction knew, it was chiefly the financials that supported the sale price.

Morgan Stanley was able to find another buyer and adjust the sale price to reflect the correct audits. The Howlands lost about $25 million. With discovery of Montgomery being essentially judgment proof and without significant insurance coverage, the Howlands decided against suing Montgomery and never laid a claim against either the local law firm or Bundy.

Adam and Eric had learned an important lesson. They had gotten tangled up in perfecting the customary language in a sale agreement, devoting so much time and effort to getting the legal language just right that they missed the big economic point underlying all the verbiage, which was having the financial strength or insurance coverage to stand behind one's opinions.

Adam suggested to Eric that the lesson be reported to the partners, at a regular partners' lunch by Adam, and to the M&A Practice Group, at one of its regular lunch meetings by Eric.

Adam thought long and hard about how to put the matter to his partners. He felt to some uncertain degree responsible for missing the point, but the prospect of the humiliation he would undergo, and the embarrassment, before his partners in admitting to such a costly error, penetrated his mind. He grappled with it until he rationalized his role in the auction as the limited one of only looking out for the interests of Jane Howland, and that, in so doing, with her implied consent, which he never discussed with her, he could rely on the local Ohio firm to know and properly reflect in the documents the Howland businesses. The redrafting of the Ohio firm's documents that he and Eric did was really just the mildest form of oversight, too insignificant to mention. And, so, with his mind cleared of fault, he described to his partners the transaction and its important lessons for the future, laying the blame for missing the question of insurance on the Ohio firm alone.

Eric's mind required no gymnastics to lay out to the M&A Practice Group the Ohio transactions and the Bundy role in them. His conclusion was short. "We fucked up in missing the question of insurance. In the future, I think the lesson is to think through not only the facts being represented and warranted, but what might happen if those facts are wrong. We checked out all the toilets without even thinking about the septic."

Adam was in the room to hear Eric's account. He wrestled to ground an immediate impulse to deny any screw-up. He would point out the fact that they had no familiarity with the Montgomery firm, unlike the local law firm chiefly responsible for the Holland interests, and therefore could reasonably assume the law firm had satisfied itself on the question of whether Montgomery had adequate financial resources, whether on its balance sheet or through insurance, to back up its opinions. But Adam knew this was grasping at straws, because he knew the Bundy approach to practice would necessarily encompass diligent inquiry on that question, even if the assignment was just oversight. And more on the point, the Bundy ethos, as repeatedly expressed by the partners in interviewing students graduating from law school and considering a position at Bundy, involved the claim of a working environment in which error could be admitted freely within client teams where 'intellectual undressing' was expected and made comfortable, all in service to the client and the vital process of learning from mistakes to master the trade. Too often to count, Adam had preached to job applicants this scripture. And Eric had just demonstrated how well he had digested the firm ethos. No wonder, recalling this incident, Adam felt guilt deep down in his gut.

The change in their status at the firm didn't change the custom Andy and Adam had developed of working late and catching a meal at the Brasserie before trudging home. If anything, the practice grew as demands at home diminished with their respective children aging into the teens. One night in 1978 they were joined at the Brasserie by Eric Slattery, who had been helping Adam on an insurance company loan. As they plowed through their soups and burgers, Eric invited them to join him at a loft party he was going to attend that evening.

"I think you'd find it interesting. Hosts are among those 'beautiful people' of the City—transplants from San Paolo, here with nothing better to do than throw parties and look for fun."

The loft was in an old West Village warehouse converted into expensive condos. They emerged from the cab to see a group of smartly dressed men and women entering the building.

"We're not dressed for this sort of thing," Andy said. "I mean, look at us. Three boring Wall Street lawyers, exhausted from the day's work, clothed in wrinkled gray suits, slightly soiled."

"Not to worry. These folks welcome all types. I guarantee we won't be the only tired lawyers in the room."

The loft was large. Rooms leading into rooms. Soft music, the hum of conversation and multitudes of people, standing, sitting, smoking, drinking and, naturally, watching each other.

On every table in every room Adam saw a bowl of manicured weed, beside which was an opened package of multicolored paper and a rolling device designed to enable even a finger-clumsy tyro to roll a serviceable joint. It was the casualness of it all that surprised Adam and Andy. They shared a sense that their world of the law was not *the World,* the one where they now found themselves, feeling more like spectators than participants, not unwelcome but not part of the scene.

Drinks were passed by waiters in white coats and black bow ties. Blacks and whites; women and men. They offered champagne and wines of white and red, all top-rated as a sip would confirm. On a stand in each room fresh shrimp were offered, together with oysters, mussels and clams on the half shell.

Eric seemed to know half the room. Especially the half Adam could see, plain enough, to be homosexuals, many sporting open-collared shirts with short sleeves and gym-bought muscles. And, why hadn't Adam expected this scene, since he had known two things about Eric from the day he started with Bundy. One, that he was from the world of 'beautiful people.' And two, immediately after observing Eric's lean taut body, his broad smile and his aura of avid sexuality, that he was a homosexual. Despite this, he had never mentioned the subject to Eric. Nor had Eric ever broached with

Adam the possibility of his being gay. Eric felt some vibes when working with Adam, but no clear signal. Nor could there have been a strong signal, since Adam was still in a state of ambiguity, despite having been married for 16 years with a son just a few years shy of college age.

As an hour passed, and then another, Adam flew higher and higher on joints, a drug he had no experience with. Andy bowed to sleep and went home. Adam was about to follow Andy out the door when fate in the person of Eric intervened. Eric had joined up with a couple of buddies to head for a disco in the meat-packing district. Before following Andy out the door with a different purpose in mind, Eric spoke to Adam, venturing the thought that he might want to join them.

"An experience," he said.

Adam's defenses against the kind of temptation Eric was offering would normally have protected him. But his mind seemed to be anaesthetized in a fog of marijuana smoke. "Yes, an experience. Why not?"

Eric led the way into a huge disco in a run-down warehouse. Adam saw hundreds of guys dancing under black light, which turned their pale torsos tan, their white T-shirts an odd shade of blue. The music was controlled by a disc-jockey in a glass booth. It flowed from one turntable to another, seamlessly, so the drug-induced frenzy could proceed, uninterrupted. Joints, Quaaludes and wine were passed along the edges of the dancing crowd. On a dais, a go-go boy in a white towel was dancing.

Adam felt himself poised at the top of a slope too steep and slippery to descend in safety. And, yet, taking a Quaalude, he began to slide down. He danced with one of Eric's friends, a guy around 30 named Benedict. He had deep circles under his eyes, the sort that priests used to ascribe to masturbation. He took off his shirt, disclosing a body hardened to a fine edge with a well turned waist, appearing brown in the black light. Adam was launched on a Roman-candle high induced by the popper, dancing crazily with Benedict, who began to talk about his 'good' 'dick', a play on his name that caused him to laugh as they throbbed to the music and to the tight embrace holding them together. Soon, he stopped jabbering about his name, and neither of them spoke, as though afraid to cut the growing sexual tension with aimless chitchat. Adam felt sheer erotic energy pulsing through his body, building up like static in a carpet. The music paused, giving Benedict the chance to take Adam's hand and lead him into one of the many little rooms surrounding the disco hall. There he pulled Adam's pants down, his underwear too, and said "Bend over, I'm going to fuck you."

Adam felt a jolt of pleasure in being dominated, so much so that he lingered after Benedict had come, taking what seemed minutes until he realized the drill. He was expected to follow suit. Afterwards, he wondered at both the simple joy and complex satisfaction of the experience. And the speed of the entire exercise. Later he would ponder the possibility that male sex was an appetite that must be fed, if not every day, then as often as possible. He feared the dangers of the road he had just begun to travel down. He realized that the promiscuity of the bath houses was a freeway to hell. But when the drug effects wore off, he put that fear aside, confident the evening had been a one-off he would not be repeating. No fall from grace, he assured himself. No loss of self-control.

In the months and years ahead, Adam's confidence proved to be a colossal misjudgment.

❧ 13 ☙

1985

The 23rd. For Liz and Adam, not like their previous wedding anniversaries, where, amidst amazement, laughter and hugs, they had joyously renewed the timeless vow 'to have and to hold, from this day forward, for better or worse, for richer or poorer, in sickness and in health, to love and to cherish, till death do us part.' Or the complimentary vow that, two decades ago, Adam was heard by the assemblage to affirm: his intention 'to love Liz, honor, and keep her in sickness and in health, and forsaking all others, keep himself only unto her, so long as they both shall live.'

Following that anniversary, Liz's confrontation and Adam's confession, they began the fraught process of untangling the braids of marriage that for two decades had bound them together.

At breakfast, Liz said, "I think, for now, I've put my anger in the bureau drawer, tucked under some sweaters, hidden enough for me to face you. We need time to talk. Tonight's as good a time as any."

"I'll be home. Count on it."

Adam walked through the door at 7:00. Liz saw him through the windows. "Aren't you missing something," she said, as he closed the door and moved to give her the hug she deftly avoided.

"Oh, you mean my briefcase. Left it in the office. On purpose. I'm serious about this—this urgency of us."

He opened a bottle of Santa Margherita's *Pinot Grigio,* grabbed a couple of glasses and sat down with her at the dining room table.

"So, how long ago did you discover you preferred men to women?"

Adam recoiled at the unexpected question, then relaxing as his mind gripped the idea that the question was 100% appropriate. Still, he was slow to answer.

"I've got to get one thing off the table. My being gay, becoming gay, whenever and however it developed, has nothing to do with you. I don't mean that. I mean you as an attractive woman, the woman I chose to marry, and have loved from the beginning, and continue to love. And been faithful to."

Adam had been speaking to his cup of coffee, head down, elbows on the table, hands on his chin.

"Faithful?" Liz felt anger escaping from her bureau to lodge deep in her throat.

"Yes, to you as a woman. The only woman in my life. Look, don't think I haven't struggled with this. How to talk about it. I guess I see it this way. Love is different from sexual preference and desire, whatever the source. Inherited or not. I cannot imagine any woman I could find more desirable than you. That's been true from the get-go. As it is today. But I have finally, and it took a long time, I have come to accept the fact, and admit it to you, that I desire men more. This is hard for me to say. And it hurts me. I'm sure it hurts you even more. Looking way back, growing up, I was molded by my parents, by the society they moved in, to find girls desirable, and I did. It was by convention, not conviction. At first, I fit the mold. Gradually, it began to pinch. Over time, I eased out of it."

Liz was in tears. "And here we are. I must say I'm moved. I appreciate your honesty. Your sensitivity to our—what to call it—to our plight. So, you have Bernie and I have our son, George. Now what? We move to separation and divorce, that's what. But I have more questions. When did you start cheating on me? No, that's not right. Cheating's not what you've been up to. Something I don't have a word for, in the context of marriage."

"It started back in '81 when I went to a fancy party in the Village. You might remember it was the night I didn't come home till dawn, claiming a super-heavy night of work. That was the first time I admitted to being hugely attracted to men. To myself. The closet break-out in the City was everywhere apparent. From Stonewall in '69 onward, the gay liberation movement had slowly gotten under my skin. From that pot-driven all-nighter on, I felt dragged into it—by forces beyond my control, genes perhaps, who knows—but I knew a change in my sexual desires had occurred. Or perhaps just an acceptance of desires that had always been there, under the surface."

"I remember. But, when you rolled into bed, you made love." It had been surprisingly good, she recalled, and remembering made her anger swell up again.

"Oh, yes. I was still high on pot and Quaaludes. They made me horny. I was high and horny—right up to dawn."

Liz suddenly realized she was last in a line of who knows how many partners that night, all male. She felt used. And not only that night. She pulled her hair from the barrettes keeping it neatly arranged and messed it up with both hands, a sure sign of deep agitation to those who know Liz well.

"Pour me some more wine."

Adam pulled the cork on a second bottle of wine, which opened up more than the bottle, loosening their tongues and cutting through the tension, keeping Liz's anger at bay, easing her humiliation and sadness, dulling those feelings enough to allow their kind of love, what could best be described as friendship deepened through living together through good times and bad, to creep in and guide the conversation. With further questioning, Adam traced his migration through various Village bath houses. Before reaching the Mine Shaft, the most exotic and frenzied spot for anonymous sex, Adam explained he found Bernie Kraus and they became partners. That was in '81.

"I know this is hard for you to take. I imagined the damage my story would cause. I can see it in your eyes."

Like a circus juggler, Liz was struggling to balance sadness and anger, to keep them fenced in, to deny either one the power to overwhelm her.

I'm sure you can. But I'm okay. Go on."

"Before Bernie, I equated sexual freedom with freedom itself. I considered having sex a positive good. And, as someone explained it, 'the more we scratched, the more we itched.' Previously guilt-ridden guys who had been seeing shrinks to eliminate that itch and remain straight in peace dropped the shrink and joined the movement. The Village was filled with gays so exuberant they were like straight sailors getting off a ship after a long voyage. You know, one of every four males in Manhattan is a homosexual."

In the telling, Adam avoided what went on in the sex centers. He was sure Liz would not want to have made concrete what she shied away from even imagining.

Poignantly, Lis responded, again unconsciously messing with her hair. "Yours was a freedom I never granted." Her voice rose, keeping pace with the anger swelling up in her throat. "And didn't know about." Now she was shouting. "You betrayed me, both sexually and emotionally. Someone needs to rewrite those marriage vows we took. They don't cover change of preference."

"From the start I felt guilty. And, at times, often actually, I felt the shame of having surrendered my integrity to the closet. I felt pulled in different directions. The guilt, the fear of hurting you by coming out pitted against the growing desire to express myself as a gay man, whether in the closet or out. For a long time they offset one another. I knew I had to come clean with you, stop the deception, but I kept putting it off. Out of fear."

Liz was confused. "Fear of what?"

"Oh, lots of things. Fear of your reaction, and George's, fear of uncertainty of the change it would cause. Fear, too, of how my partners would react. And Father."

"That fear excused you." She felt the anger grow, more intense than before, as she had suddenly remembered the risk of infection. "It allowed you to continue to betray me, to abdicate responsibility. It's just not acceptable. And you exposed me to AIDS! Without my even knowing. It's practically criminal!"

"I thought we covered that. You know I haven't been diagnosed. Look, you know I became monogamous two years ago, that Bernie and I are clean, that we trust—we believe—each other. We didn't change because of AIDS. In '81, we didn't really understand the disease. We were up to here with the anonymous sex life in the Village. More than enough. For us the 'noble experiment', you know, of separating the sensual from the emotional, of having sex as often as one can. With as many partners as one can. All that was over. As Bernie put it the night we had that beer together, the bath houses were both an escape from loneliness and a guarantee of loneliness. Whatever AIDS was—and in '81 we didn't have much of a clue—we were sure it wasn't divine punishment for the sin of same-sex love. That 'wrath of God' stuff was repulsive nonsense—probably started in the White House."

Liz was able, again, to throttle down her anger.

"So, I know I shouldn't ask, but I have to. Want to tell me how you met Bernie?"

"We met at the St. Mark's bathhouse. We just sort of bumped into each other exiting the place. Bernie looked at me, up and down. Then he said 'Man, you look drained. Just the way I feel. How 'bout a drink?' I looked at his face. I saw honesty and a hunger for something he hadn't found in St. Mark's. Call it friendship. I said 'sure.' We went to a nearby bar. We had a couple of drafts. We talked, exchanging stories about who we were. And who we thought we were. And who we wanted to be. We were there a long time. We left as friends."

"Was it then that you stopped going to the bathhouses?"

Adam stood. "Have to pee. I'll be right back, and answer your question."

Returning, he slid into his chair and poured himself another glass of wine.

"Thanks. Yes, that was when we stopped. Sitting in the bar, we looked at each other and saw the same thing. A yearning unsatisfied by anonymous sex. It was as if the exhilaration of being gay, feeling the freedom of release from the closeted life, and wallowing in it, had worn itself out. We discovered so much in common. The same needs tugging. We confessed a desire for something else. A relationship. A bond that would last. Something more than the sex. In exiting the bathhouse that night, bumping into each other on the way out, having a few drafts, we uncovered something. We wanted to quit the way we were living."

Liz poured herself more wine. Pushing her threshold for pain, she went deeper. "So, who is he?"

Adam poured himself another glass, draining the bottle. He felt loose, tipsy.

"Bernie's an artist. He makes his bread that way. He's an accomplished artist. He's a kind and thoughtful man." Adam paused to examine Liz's expression.

"Okay, but give me more."

"Bernie's the son of Jews from Krakow, who slipped the Nazi noose to end up first in Argentina, and finally in Brooklyn, where he grew up. His father's a postman and a loving parent. His mother kept house. She was extreme in her ambition for Bernie. Sometimes, he allowed, it was embarrassing. He has an older brother, a psychiatrist, who uncovered the fact that Bernie was gay but kept Bernie's secret from his parents until 1973. He knew they'd be devastated. I discovered all this before we'd finished our first glass of beer. It seemed to ignite some mutual feelings."

"Why 1973?"

"Yeah, good question. Therein lies a tale of its own. It was the year in which the American Psychiatric Association declassified homosexuality as a mental illness. Bernie's brother had accepted his profession's opinion, despite it's being rooted in prejudice rather than science, until this official change freed him to follow his instincts. For he had never accepted as fact that Bernie was mentally ill. He now felt free to encourage Bernie to come out, at least to his parents and perhaps to others."

"Wasn't there some lag time between this change and the explosion of gays coming out?"

"We're getting away from who Bernie is. But, in fact, he explained the astounding tale of how the change occurred. I think you'd appreciate this. At the previous year's APA conference, a 34-year old gay psychiatrist, concealed in oversized clothes and a rubber mask and wig, appeared on stage, identified himself as "Henry Anonymous, M.D., and rocked the meeting by describing the secret world of gay psychiatrists. Secret because disclosure for a gay psychiatrist would result in revocation of license, loss of career. But an even greater loss to gay doctors, he said, was the loss of their honest humanity. For decades no one knew the identity of this psychiatrist. But his goal, the declassification of homosexuality, was achieved one year later, in 1973."

"What a story! One isolated event and the world changed." Liz had grabbed another bottle of wine to open. Shame and anger had both retreated to some closet in her wine-infused brain.

"No more for me, Liz. Back to Bernie. He attended local high school, excelled in course work, got hooked in an extracurricular art course. Got a scholarship to Pratt and studied to be a portrait artist. He did portraits of his father and mother. Despite being praised by professors at Pratt, those paintings, which he had hoped would be the passage to a career in portrait art, led nowhere after graduating. I mean nowhere in that exclusive, haphazard world of portraiture. As he put it, 'a Brooklyn Jew with no connections—forget about it.'

My own take, having known Bernie a couple of years, is that he's too self-contained, shy and honest to be, or even try to be, successful in this field. Not charming or self-promotional enough to get hired by dealers or the type of rich client who wants his portrait, or that of his family, painted. He needed a patron saint. But he never found one. Instead, he found work doing book covers for big publishers. I see tragedy in his career. He's a brilliant artist and deserves better. And, by the way, he's doing a portrait of me."

"Really?" she said, suddenly feeling lonely and morose. And, yet, like a battered fighter, she couldn't stop staggering forward, asking for more. "Did your friendship migrate to love?"

"Yes. We found a passion for each other within a week of that bump at the bathhouse door. But it came wrapped in friendship—a caring for each other, something neither of us had experienced with men before. A caring like I have for you and for George. I found room for more, and with that caring came the electricity. We both felt it."

Liz stood, feeling wrung out. Again, she thought of the virus. "I'm leaving you to go to bed. Before I go, about AIDS, and just to be clear, bottom line, you're not worried about it. You're safe."

"Absolutely," Adam replied, looking up into her sad, still wet eyes. "More importantly, you're safe."

Spinning around towards the door, she exclaimed with a soft growl, "That's good to hear."

Adam sat for a while, finishing the wine in his glass. He hated himself for the damage obviously done to Liz. He sensed she might actually be jealous of Bernie, as plausible from her questions and demeanor as it was, from his perspective, absurd. He knew he had room for her friendship beside Bernie's. He just had to find a way to convince her. And then he remembered George. Explaining the whole sorry saga was not going to be easy. He knew he would need Liz to help, and keeping her friendship was going to be a prerequisite. He dreaded the talk with George.

❦

Adam called his mother to ask if he could come to their house for dinner.

"We're free next week, most nights. How's Wednesday, at six. You and Liz for dinner. It seems like ages since we last saw you. What a treat," Hannah trilled.

"Liz can't make it, mother. Just me."

"Well, dear, why don't we pick a night when she's free. We'd like to see you both, of course."

Adam was annoyed. Something he hadn't anticipated. "Look, mother, I want to talk about our marriage, and other things, and it is better I do it alone."

"As you wish, Adam. But now I'm alarmed. Do you want to tell me now? Okay, no need to get angry. We will look forward to seeing you next Wednesday."

Off to a bad start, he feared, recognizing he must have sounded petulant.

Adam arrived at his parents' door in Mamaroneck on time. Their welcome was unnaturally effusive, as if they were desperate to show parental love and acceptance, no matter what. It was obvious to Adam that they sensed his problems and, despite knowing nothing, wanted to signal they were on his side. He felt the prodigal son.

Over drinks, they caught up with one another on all matters immaterial to Adam's visit. They didn't push him, tiptoeing around the conversation as if they were trying to take an egg from under a hen without her noticing.

When Hannah had served dinner's main course and seated herself, Adam began.

"Liz and I are separating. We will get a divorce. It's all amicable and, we believe, should not be painful to George. By the way, he doesn't know. We thought it best to tell him when he's home for Thanksgiving, face to face."

Hannah felt immense sadness. And worry. She marveled at his apparent lack of emotion. Long had she wondered about Adam's state of mind, his marriage, his happiness. Although she didn't see him often, they talked almost weekly on the phone. And she spoke by phone with Liz, although not as often. Gradually she got the sense something was slightly out of plumb, like a painting hanging askew, something lurking behind Adam's intensity and overwhelming devotion to hours spent in the office. And something about the narrowing range of subjects Liz seemed open to discussing. Hannah's sense from these calls was of a loving parent whose desire to express motherly understanding and sympathy for whatever was going on with Adam and Liz was being denied to her. Without cause or reason. She knew in her bones that her son was repressing emotions that, one way or another, like water against gravity, would find a way out.

Wright looked his son in the eye and said, "Why?"

"I'm a homosexual. It's taken me half a lifetime to uncover this fact, but finally, I've admitted it to myself—accepted it—as true. I've told Liz. She's trying hard to be understanding. But it's going to take time. As it will with you."

Wright recoiled, pain drenching his reddening face. He stood.

"How could this happen? After the way we raised you? The molding to make us proud of you. After all we've done. This is inconceivable for a son of mine."

"Father, please listen to me. There's more to say."

Wright turned away from the table. "I've heard all I want. You've done enough damage to your family already. It is unforgiveable." He moved swiftly up the stairs to his bedroom.

Wright's behavior had rendered a verdict more powerful than words could support. He had closed his ears to the news, batting it away like an annoying fly, and by his swift retreat, assuring that Adam understood he would no longer be welcome in his father's house.

Catching each other's eyes, seeing the pained expressions, Hannah and Adam looked away, staring at their empty dinner plates.

Hannah was no fan of homosexuals. Adam's news shocked her. Just as shocking as it was to Wright, but one hundred and eighty degrees different. Instead of blaming Adam for his homosexuality, and thinking of damage to the family, she blamed herself and Wright, and thought of Adam's pain, as well as Liz's and George's, looking down the road. Later, in bed that night, thinking it over, again and again, the shock wore off and with it some of the guilt. She thought of all the famous homosexuals, from Oscar Wilde to Gore Vidal. And so many others. These associations eased her mind. They all had mothers. Mothers who loved them. Why not Adam, she thought, and why not me. Always the optimist, no matter how unrealistic, she drifted off to sleep.

Liz and Adam separated and put in train the steps to divorce. Together, over Thanksgiving Day weekend, when George came home from Cornell, where he was in sophomore year, they sat down with him in the kitchen to explain their plans and the underlying cause. It was not an easy discussion, since, so carefully had Adam guarded his other life that George had no inkling of that life or of his mother's reaction to it. For what seemed an eternity, he sat silent, looking first at Adam and then at Liz.

"I feel like a tsunami of a wave has just smacked me in the face. It's unimaginable, this story. I'd think you were joking if it weren't so obvious from your faces that this is for real. But Dad, how could you have married Mom if you were a homosexual? It's disgusting. I don't know what more to say."

Liz said "George, we loved each other when we courted and married. We've continued to love one another. Love has many meanings. We're separating so we each can live our own lives, and be true to ourselves. And to you. And our friendship will continue. That's a given. And our love for you, that continues. It's all okay. It's all going to be okay."

"I hear you. But I can't accept it. I was conceived as part of a fiction."

Liz said, "Adam didn't know when we married. He didn't deceive me, or himself. It was only recently that he discovered his sexuality. Isn't that right, Adam?"

"More or less." Adam was thinking hard. He began to speak slowly, deliberately and with intensity. "Look, you are not part of some fiction, as you put it. You're our son. Conceived through our love for one another. You grew up in a loving family. You've said as much, yourself. More than once. I think we'd best adjourn this discussion. Give yourself some time. And give us some time too. It's a big deal and deserves some time out for each of us to think the whole thing over."

George stood up, walked to a large photograph on the wall and took it down. It was a picture of his parents on either side of their son at his third birthday party, watching as he tried to blow out the candles on the cake in front of him. Written below in gold lettering appeared the words: "The Happy Hudsons on George's Third Birthday."

"Look at this picture. It's a fraud. You know, Dad, growing up, and even now, how much I've wanted to be like you, because of the Dad you've been. You've been there for me, always, and I felt it. Even when you missed dinner, working in the office. I always felt you were open, honest with Mom and with me, putting in office time because it was your profession, and it was for us. I admired you. But, now it all seems like a lie, like you deceived us. You're right. It is a big deal."

Heading upstairs to his room, George left his parents behind in the kitchen, where they tried to sort things out.

Liz said, "I understand his anger. It's going to take time, and a lot of talking, to reel him in. You answered him well. But I don't think he really heard you. We've got to listen to him."

"Yeah, and be completely honest. That's been the problem. I wasn't honest with myself, and that made it hard to be honest with you and George."

"I get that, but for several years you practiced deception. To restore George's trust, you've got to speak to him about that. It can't just be erased, or covered over. It's a fact we all have to live with."

George's closest friend at Cornell was Peter Lindabury, a quiet fellow given to hard thinking and sparse talk. They each had a single room on the same floor of a Sophomore dorm. George discovered that, when he spoke, Peter often expressed surprising insights, whatever the topic. George found him immensely good company, exceptionally smart in an unassuming way, easy to be with, comfortable in sharing confidences.

On returning to campus after Thanksgiving, and without planning to do so, over beers one night he told Peter the devastating news about his father.

"I feel like I've been stabbed in the back. How could he do this to us?"

Peter seemed unfazed by Adam's revelation. He looked into Adam's eyes, then turned to stare at his half-full glass of beer, deep in thought.

"So, George, since you shared your story, I will share mine. I'm a homosexual. I don't broadcast the fact, but I have no shame about it. That's who I am. Now, knowing this fact, do you like me any less? I hope not." George, recovering from the shock, shook his head.

"And so, my point is that there is no reason to like your father any less either. I'm sure he had reasons for keeping his homosexuality a secret, as do I. Society isn't entirely comfortable with us, yet. As to whether you yank me out of the closet or not, I ask simply that you use discretion and common sense. A number of people know I'm gay."

"Including your parents?"

"Yes. They sensed it before I laid it on the table. They've been a source of understanding and support. Perhaps, as you think the whole thing through, and come to grips, this is the sort of thing you might offer your father. The job, and it's a big one, is to try to put yourself in your father's shoes."

"But he deceived my mother and me. He was living a secret life."

"Do you know when he knew he was a homosexual? It might have only happened long after his marriage and your birth. There are so many questions to pursue if you want to be fair in trying to get into your father's shoes. I think the first step for you is to replace your anger with curiosity, with an openness to being surprised. Let's have another round."

"Okay, curiosity. When did you know you were gay?"

"Oh, I knew from a young age. I knew in grade school, as puberty began. I had strong feelings for certain boys in my school. Physical attractions. At first they confused me. I thought them contrary to the natural order of things. For magnets, likes repel. If all men were homosexuals, the race would peter out. Wasn't this contrary to Darwinian theories? I started to read about homosexuality. Books by Larry Kramer and Edmund White. I discovered a whole world out there, one to which I could belong. Reading about homosexuals by homosexuals was a comfort. So, I went to my parents with the big disclosure, only to find they had already guessed. Society today is much more accepting than when your father was growing up. I urge you not to rush to judgment. The subject is riddled with complexity, and everyone has his own unique story. You've just opened the cover on your father's."

George was moved by the power of Peter's wisdom and advice. Reflecting on the evening's conversation, George realized Peter was advanced in his thought processes both in the sense of his age and his time. George thought it possible that Peter had just enabled him to turn a corner or at least start down the road toward understanding and acceptance.

$$\text{❧ 14 ❧}$$

1985-1989

From the separation on, slowly at first, but then more swiftly, Adam felt an enormous weight he had long suffered under being removed, brick by brick, as if by magic. He began robustly to expand in many directions that were not new to him but had been covered over, like the heavy fall of leaves in November, by his effort to live in skin not quite his own, a skin that, for two decades and more, didn't fit, that he knew restrained him not from rectitude and professionalism but from the joyful parts of his personality, from the playful. It was a skin he couldn't shed until released by the truth Liz uncovered. At the time, a disaster. In hindsight, a fortuitous accident.

In the office, he grew in empathy for his partners and associates, not by loosening his discipline or the famed precision in his work, but by adding an element of compassion and concern for his colleagues that had not always been evident in earlier times.

He recaptured his love for singing by rejoining the West Side Community Chorale, a leading amateur chorus in the City led by Byard Scott, a group with high standards that attracted singers who considered the chorus the most important avocational activity in their busy lives. It was a chorus he had sung with upon arriving in the City, but soon found he couldn't handle, given other demands.

And then, with Bernie, he took increasing delight in cooking. In the kitchen he revealed, in a new way, the sense of precision and order that lawyers working with him had come to view as commonplace. He mastered a full range of recipes and became exceedingly particular as to how things should proceed in the kitchen, to the point of absurd insistence, behavior Bernie had limited patience for. At first, they argued over things as simple as how to boil an egg. Adam's certainty on matters culinary would have been funny, but for the fact that Bernie was not only knowledgeable but experienced in the kitchen and unwilling to be pushed around. After many collisions of will, Adam seemed to relax, grow less insistent and back off, often with grace and a chuckle of self-awareness.

"Bernie, I'm being an ass again."

One night Adam planned butternut squash with ginger and green curry soup, from a recipe he had seen in the *NY Times*. Using a peeler, Adam had just removed the skin from the squash when Bernie came into the kitchen. The peels were stacked neatly in a pile, all virtually the same in width and length.

Looking at them, Bernie remembered Adam's impossibly anal way with artichoke leaves, a practice learned growing up and continued into maturity and beyond.

"Adam, I told you what a new man you've become since the separation. More than once. But not everything's changed. Your discipline in disposing of spent artichoke leaves, and now I see with squash skin. Unaffected. A remnant of the old man. Wow!"

Smiling broadly, Adam said: "No comment."

1985 turned out to be a memorable year. In April, Larry Kramer's play, *The Normal Heart,* opened at The Public Theatre, in a widely celebrated production by Joseph Papp. Reviews heralded the play as a masterpiece of political drama. Kramer had depicted AIDS not as the wrath of God but the wrath of heterosexuals. Writing for the NY Daily News, Liz Smith called it "An astounding drama ... a damning indictment of a nation in the middle of an epidemic with its head is the sand. It will make your hair stand on end even as the tears spurt from your eyes."

And then, on October 2, Rock Hudson, the essence of screen projected masculinity, died of AIDS. By that date 12,000

Americans were dead or dying from the disease, while hundreds of thousands had been infected.

On reading the news, Bernie said "Adam, we should go to *The Normal Heart*."

"I've thought about that. I know Kramer's message, and it doesn't apply to us. We don't have AIDS, we've put pursuit of sexual liberation behind us, we've got each other. It would not only be painful but inapposite. You know, it ends with Kramer's alter ego marrying his lover in a hospital bed, moments before the lover dies from AIDS."

"You've got a point. I'm dropping that idea. Let's find a comedy instead."

As the months passed, Bernie marveled at what he saw happening in slow motion right before his eyes. Caterpillar to butterfly. Adam took wing, becoming a man at ease with himself and those around him. He grew more relaxed, experimental and even became free from the need—his original sin—always to get things right the first time—or put differently, never being able to say simply 'I fucked up.' In their apartment, especially in the kitchen, but elsewhere as well, Adam was heard to say precisely that, and then laugh at himself. His personality was becoming, in Bernie's sharp eye, one of easy spontaneity sustained by a new-found sense of joy. Given the very limited number of times Adam made blunders, he almost seemed to relish them, calling Bernie's attention to them with a new-found pride.

From his perch, Bernie could see, almost day by day, his partner's migration. One night, after dinner and a touch more wine than was healthy, Adam stood, glass in hand. "Bernie, you've never heard me recite 'The Cremation of Sam McGee.' It's been years—decades really—since I last did it. But I feel the time has come."

With only a few rough edges, Adam plowed through the long poem with an infectious vigor. Bernie was smitten. "What a treat! Where'd you learn that?"

Adam was pleased with himself. So pleased that he was shocked to realize how long it had been since he had given to others, and received in return, the pleasures of reciting the Service poems he had memorized in high school. Why had he bottled them up for so long? He felt it had something to do with the lingering, unresolved relationship he had with his father, who had pushed him hard as a youth to put his unusual memory to good purpose. The break now seemed complete. He saw no obvious route to repair it. With this conclusion, he grew less restrained.

Bernie decided to do Adam's portrait. It would be a loving labor, a relief from the daily grind of book covers, a rendering that might survive down the years. Adam liked the idea, agreeing to the few sitting sessions required by Bernie's technique, which used photographs as well. Given Adam's skills and character, Bernie decided to give his lover the trappings of a Greek scholar, enough to conjure up a philosopher like Socrates. There was nobility about Adam's face and stature. His thick hair had receded somewhat, but it remained black, with mere brush strokes of gray and white here and there. In the toga Bernie used, he appeared ramrod upright, square shouldered and, yet, thoughtful, receptive to the ideas of others, open to challenge and debate. As close to heroic as Bernie dared essay. Such was the artist's intention, and in Adam's opinion, he succeeded brilliantly.

With the painting framed and ready to be hung, Adam asked Bernie if he regretted not having done more portraits. "You're really good, but I suppose you know that. What was the last portrait you did?"

"Oh, dear, you are opening a life-long wound. Yours is the first portrait I've done since, long ago, I painted my parents. Nothing in between except book covers. Imagine, and the only portraits were done not for loot but for love. It's the difficult and painful story of my life. By any measure within the portraiture field I'm a failure. A fact I have buried. I don't feel a failure, just unlucky. That's how I've lived with myself. And I've not always been unlucky. For God's sake no. Didn't you come along to pull me out of the baths, dry me off and hug me?

They hung the portrait in their bedroom.

One night when Bernie was bent over the stove preparing a dinner delayed by a call from Adam predicting a couple of hours more of work before he could get home, he heard on public radio a report by the CDC on the AIDS epidemic. A study of those infected with HIV by blood transfusions, which give a certain starting date for infection, indicated the mean incubation period for developing AIDS was five and a half years, with a range of from six months to eleven years or possibly even more. And, sadly, there was no reliable way to detect HIV.

When Adam returned Bernie told him about the report.

"That means we are now, June '88, just about seven years past our rambunctious period in the bathhouses. Crossed the mean, but given the range, not near the edge of the forest."

"Bernie, talk less, cook those chops more. I feel certain we are well out of the woods. We'd know by now. We both feel fine. Stop worrying, for God's sake. No, for my sake and yours."

"Okay, Okay. You always greet me with 'What news?' The CDC report is news. But I take your point. And the chops are done. If you'll set the table, we can eat."

While killing the pork chops, they spoke of their migration from acceptance of their sexuality to robust display in the baths to the partnership now so well established between them. Recalling the chapters in their story, Adam grew maudlin. "You know, Bernie, being alone in a crowd isn't necessarily the same thing as being lonely. But, looking back, my nights in the Village, surrounded by men, was the quintessence of loneliness. Ironic, no?"

"Yeah, we were searching for companionship, but in our exuberance, the path we took led only to sex and isolation. Yeah, and ultimately left us feeling lonely, even abandoned when the night was done."

There was no announcement, firm-wide or to the partners, regarding Adam's separation, divorce or new partnership with Bernard Kraus. The circle of those aware of these changes expanded slowly. Those noticing a change in Adam's personality, however, was as large as the number of lawyers with whom he had regular contact. He seemed much less intense and narrowly focused on the inhuman aspects of crafting a perfect document. He showed wider interests in his colleagues, in the non-legal aspects of their lives, in their health and in an almost unique concern for their job satisfaction, or even more surprising, their happiness and fulfillment, for which he had expanded his view of the firm to embrace as a firm responsibility along with its professional standards.

It was a delicate business, for his colleagues might read his concerns as an invasion of their privacy. But Adam was acutely aware of that line and kept back from it, even as it varied from lawyer to lawyer. He was often heard to say to lawyers who came within his circle at Bundy: "You must warm both hands on the fire of life, and that means a complete life, one that extends well beyond the confines of your practice here." Working elbow to elbow with Adam became a joy for those lucky enough to be picked, for it entailed not just a passing along of the skills of a legal practice at its peak, but passing along as well an inspiration for living a life in full, wherever one's path might lead.

One night Adam was working late with a young associate, Charlie Olsen. Adam had asked Charlie to check on New York's usury laws, as the interest rate on the loan he was working on, 12.5%, was higher than Adam had ever seen before.

Seated next to Adam at his office conference table, Charlie reported on his research.

"I believe the usury level for corporate borrowers in New York is 25%."

More than once, before Adam left his wife, young lawyers had expressed the results of their research to Adam in terms of belief. And he had cut them down. "Beliefs are for priests; lawyers think." They typically left Adam's office feeling embarrassed and humiliated, their professionalism demeaned, merely through the choice of a verb.

With Charlie, he delivered the same message, but put it in bubble-wrap to avoid breaking Charlie's spirit. "If you believe in something rather than think it true, it almost sounds like it could be different from what you believe. That word seems to offer more wiggle room than I think you intend. Am I right?"

Charlie nodded. "Yes, I get your point. A bit like talking about God. For lawyers, 'think' is the better verb."

On another occasion, Gavin Amler, an associate with several years' experience, appeared at the door of Adam's office, was invited in and sat down in the chair opposite Adam. Adam had asked him to contact a law school friend practicing in an Ohio firm and arrange with that firm to render an opinion on an acquisition of an Ohio business by a company represented by Bundy. Gavin reported that the Ohio firm would not only take on the assignment, but share 10% of the fees charged in appreciation for the referral. Gavin's face conveyed pleasure in what he had accomplished and a prideful excitement over the 10%.

Here was a sensitive subject. Adam had faced the forwarding fee issue once before, shortly after he became a partner. He had responded to a young associate's delighted report of having been offered such a fee with harshness. He charged the associate with advancing a proposal (which he called, with purpose, a 'scheme') in violation of New York's Rules of Professional Conduct. These Rules prohibit the acceptance of fees unless they are for actual work done. The associate hadn't read the Rules and didn't know of this prohibition. The way Adam scolded him made him feel morally impaired. The associate never fully recovered, leaving the firm within the next year. Now, recalling the incident, Adam felt remorse.

"Gavin, I bet you remember from your criminal law class at law school the distinction between *malum prohibitum* and *malum in se*. Well, a forwarding fee falls into the category of *malum prohibitum*. It is not an evil thing but something the legal fraternity has declared by rule to be unacceptable. The underlying theory is that lawyers should only be paid for professional services rendered. This idea isn't obvious. I'm not surprised at your delight in the offer. But,

I must disappoint you. We can't take that 10%. May I suggest you have a look at the Rules and satisfy yourself on the point."

When Gavin left, Adam pondered his handling of the matter. He knew something in him had changed, and here was an item of proof he recalled with a wince. The word 'mellow' came to mind. Yes, it captured Adam as he emerged from a life of pretend and repress.

The firm typically had a dance party every few years, booking the Rainbow Room at the top of Rockefeller Center for the purpose. Adam loved to dance, but the idea of bringing Bernie to this event raised questions. He was out in his firm and in public to the degree anyone wanted to pursue the matter. In other words, he believed, he was being honest in how he lived his life, despite being not eager to call attention to it. Bringing Bernie to the Bundy dance would be to invite knowledge and scrutiny. This he would not do. He flirted with the idea of asking Liz to join him, since he wanted to participate and enjoy the evening. Attending alone didn't feel right, given his relationships with Liz and Bernie. He finally decided against inviting Liz and against attending. To share his new life with the whole firm in one evening was going to be too heavy a burden, while going by himself seemed too lonely to stomach. And with Liz there would be the risk of misleading.

Towards the end of January of last year, Adam developed lesions on his arms, then on his legs. Bernie urged Adam to see a doctor. It took almost 12 months for Adam to pick up the phone. Finally, at Bernie's now angry insistence, he made an appointment with an AIDS specialist, who was booked into late January of '89. The timing was off for Bernie to accompany him. "I tried another time, but he's booked for months. I'll be okay."

Unhappily for Adam, the appointment occurred in the middle of the City's biggest snow storm of the season. The snow was deep, the wind wicked and the frost biting when Adam, wrapped like an Egyptian mummy in a floor length scarf, embarked for the doctor's office. The doorman got him a cab, which struggled through recently plowed snow to deliver Adam, by then in a mild state of alarm, to the right address.

The examination was swift; the conclusion unqualified. The doctor informed Adam that he had AIDS. He could have gotten infected five or more years ago. The chief uncertainty, the doctor advised, was how long Adam would live. He quoted from a CDC report of April 1983, in which, of all people diagnosed with AIDS on or before July 26, 1982, two-thirds were dead by the time of that report, nine months later. The doctor left Adam with one final thought. "Beyond the science, experience tells us that the will to live can make a big difference."

Bernie was waiting at the door of their apartment when Adam returned, sodden with snow on his exterior and fears inside. Only the snows, he realized, would melt away.

"Well?" Bernie said, his voice rising.

"It is as you thought."

Bernie broke into tears.

They cried together, standing in the foyer. Bernie took Adam's hand and led him to the kitchen table.

"What now?" said Bernie.

"We go on living. I mean… Have your read *Lord Jim*?"

"What the hell are you talking about?"

"Yes, I love that book and I've never forgotten a Conrad line:

> 'A man that is born falls into a dream like a man who falls into the sea. … The way is to the destructive element submit yourself and with the exertions of your hands and feet in the water make the deep, deep sea keep you up.'

"That's fantasy land, Adam. Get a grip."

"We shall have a dinner party. You invite two and I do the same. We will plan a menu and I will cook, with your help, of course."

Bernie perked up, catching Adam's spirit.

"The Last Supper comes to mind. Promise me you'll do 'The Shooting of Dan McGrew.'

"Ah, but of course I will. But it's no last supper. A grand dinner. And we will do this again and again."

They picked Valentine's Day for the dinner. Adam invited Charlie Pott and Roger Scragg, his most intimate buddies from Bundy who had shared his secrets while in the closet. Bernie invited two close friends, both gay. Adam's menu included his favorites: Tarragon Chicken (bone-in, skin on thighs) with sherry vinegar onions, including for additional aromatics some thyme sprigs and garlic cloves. Braised cannellini beans with Swiss chard, garlic cloves, minced rosemary, red pepper flakes, vegetable stock, onions and hashed Brussels sprouts with lemon. And for dessert, rustic olive oil cake with honey syrup.

With difficulty Bernie picked the wine, finally settling on Paul Kubler's Pinot Blanc K from Alsace. Led by Adam, they cooked the meal together. The AIDS sentence from Adam's doctor seemed to concentrate time for the couple, intensifying every feeling, deepening memory. Adam spoke for them both in saying to Bernie "I believe our feelings in the kitchen express a communion of human spirits—ones who know how to live."

"Yes, I know it sounds pretentious, but there's poetry in this kitchen."

The vibes around the dinner table on that evening could not be missed. Warm feelings enveloped the room, intoxicating the diners with friendship. Adam's cooking was justly admired as was the Alsatian wine. Adam's symptoms were there too, impossible for the guests to miss, especially when he recited the Service ballad about Dan McGrew, his voice failing him at times as he had to catch his elusive breath.

After dessert, Bernie proposed the first toast: "You all know by now Adam's love for the poems of Robert Service. Well, I looked through his copy of Selected Poems, and came across these lines from Service's poem titled 'Grin.' They fit Adam:

> "Your trouble is that you don't know when you have
>   had enough –
>
>   Don't give in.

If Fate should down you, just get up and take another cuff;
You May bank on it that there is no philosophy like bluff,
And grin.'
To my friends: good health, good life and much love."

Adam followed at greater length, with Thornton Wilder's *The Bridge of San Luis Rey* in hand, suggesting, naturally enough for him, advance preparation. He said: "The narrator in Wilder's *The Bridge* concludes his memorial to five fallen travelers with this thought:

'We ourselves shall be loved for a while and then forgotten. But the love will have been enough. Even memory is not necessary for love. There is a land of the living and a land of the dead and the bridge is love …'

The guests rose and, with strong hugs all around, departed. Outside, they were greeted by a crisp cold wind, driving dry snow, inches of fluffy silver crystals accumulated on the sidewalks and on the yet to be plowed streets.

New lesions, lungs filling with protozoa, eternally tired without reason. He gradually turned the clients he was responsible for over to others. News of his affliction, like a whirlpool in reverse, swiftly flowed outward from the firm's leaders to all who knew Adam. He clung to rehearsals for *Life and Death in the Time of AIDS*. Through the week, he would bank his energy, hoping to draw down a surplus to use on Tuesday night, when the Chorus rehearsed for two and more hours in the St. Ignatius Church on West End Avenue. As the weeks passed, standing to rehearse became too taxing. Byard arranged a chair for Adam, who for moments flinched at the idea of being the only sitting chorister, but then accepted, and soon embraced it. He came to believe he was Exhibit A to the concert's theme. For his part, Byard never put the question to Adam. He knew, and Adam knew he knew, wondering for how long?

The chorus performed *In the Time of AIDS* on a Friday night and Sunday afternoon in late May. It was the first of its kind. Byard had attracted to the concert not only Randy Shilts, Edmund White and Larry Kramer, but a reporter from the Times. The Bundy firm was well represented in the audience. The church was full for both performances, with many forced to turn away. Bernie attended both performances, friends in tow. A reception was held in the crypt of the church on Sunday evening, after which Byard joined Adam, his friends Charlie and Roger, and Bernie for an effulgent dinner at Carmine's.

Byard was ecstatic.

"A grand concert. Adam, you and the others outdid yourselves! Hey, there, you look positively beat."

Adam nodded, too spent to talk.

Bernie said, "Adam stored his energy to get through these concerts. I'm sure, when he recovers with some wine and food, he will confirm his reserve was exhausted, and then some."

Adam smiled. A cold Pinot Grigio was poured. They raised their glasses to toast the concert. Adam drank deeply and then whispered: "That's the most moving thing I've been part of—ever."

"It was your concert as much as mine," said Byard. "A toast to you my friend."

As glasses were raised in his honor, Adam fell asleep. And, waking enough to climb in a cab, he fell asleep again on the way home.

❦ 15 ❦

1989-1990

He called Liz to report on the state of matters and see if she might like to visit. Although he tried to dismiss it, having denied the risk so often and so vigorously, and having been backed 100% by Bernie, he now worried. Having long ago convinced Liz that she was okay, with his declining condition seizing his mind, he began to worry that, in fact, he had infected Liz.

"Hello, Adam. It's so good to hear from you. We scooted out quickly when the concert ended, but George and I were there on Friday. We both thought it just magnificent. Congratulations. So many of those pieces got to me, down deep in the center of things. Especially *Crossing the Bar*. No, not that alone. All of them. We're you pleased?"

"Yes, very happy. Quite a thrill. So glad you came, and George too. Liz, I'm calling to update you on my condition. It's AIDS. No question about it. I guess you saw how I looked at the concert. I don't know how long I've got. I seem to be weakening. Perhaps you'd drop by. I'd like that. And George when he's around."

"I'll be there. I'm sure George will want to see you. I think you know he came to grips with our divorce. More important, he accepted your homosexuality. It's been an impressive migration. But, I think it best we do separate visits. He should have time with you alone. I'll have a word with him. What about your parents? Are they up to date?"

"Do you remember Father wouldn't allow me to tell him I was a homosexual. Wouldn't hear me trying to explain the cause of our separation? Now, tell me, what should I do? Not to be able to talk with him is painful. But more painful still, much more, is rejection, trying to talk and having him close his ears and mind to me."

"Adam, I'd like to advise you. And I would if I had any good insight. But it's too personal a matter—personal to you—I dare not venture in."

When Liz came to visit, Adam had been to see his father, after being pushed hard by Bernie to do so.

"It was ugly, Liz. I felt unwanted by him. He seemed too embarrassed by me to want to hear. He spoke of me as a teenager who had disappointed him in various ways. The markings I tried to leave on his blackboard he would have erased by the time I passed out his office door."

"That's awful. It's too, too painful. I think of the hurt a person suffers from being cut out of a will. That's nothing compared to your father's rejection. That man's deficient in kindness. It's gross.

"I wasn't going to tell you this, but now I guess I should. I tried hard to get your parents to come to the AIDS concert, going out to see them at home. I pleaded, saying how important it was to you and how surprised and pleased you'd be if they were there. My pleading found a deaf ear in Dwight, who said 'The whole idea is foreign and distasteful. Adam, my son, your former husband, has abandoned us both. He's gone down a path I refuse to follow.' We argued. To make matters worse, Hannah said she wanted to go and Dwight forbade her, right there in front of me. I got so angry I asked Dwight why he couldn't show a little kindness and respect. Of course, it was a rhetorical question. I felt I had blown it. I left in frustration with myself. And anger at your father."

"Thanks, Liz, for trying, for the thought behind the effort. I could have predicted the outcome. Will George come by?"

Yes, he'll call before."

"Tell him I count on his visit. Anytime. I'm not going anywhere."

Bernie met George at the door. They went into the bedroom where Adam lay, snoozing.

"George is here to see you."

Adam opened his eyes, grasped the message and sat up to extend his hand to George, who grasped it solidly in his own before bending over to give Adam a long hug.

On both their minds, meshing in silence like well-oiled gears, was the fleeting thought that, possibly, they would not be seeing one another again. One could curse it, but AIDS was immune to feelings. They both felt its presence.

Bernie said "I think I'll leave you two Hudson boys to yourselves. Call if you need anything."

"You make me happy being here, George. Thanks. I've been thinking a lot about my life, my marriage and the wonderful thing that happened when you came into our lives. It's all very confusing now, looking back. I screwed things up for you and Liz, and I want to apologize for that, for hiding in the closet, for not being honest with you both, or with myself. But then, I think about the costs of honesty. No marriage and no you. And when I think of that, I shy away—not from apologies but from regrets. I have only a deepening sadness over the hard fact of my sexuality, over the many years it took me to accept the reality and the consequences that followed—inexorably it seemed—given the times we lived through. And, now, AIDS. It's hard not to view the disease as a form of punishment."

Adam's chain of thought had set George crying. "You have nothing to be punished for. I don't believe in divine retribution. You know it took me some time to come to terms with the separation. But I did. Helped by the chance discovery at school that one of my closest friends was gay. He administered strong advice about wearing your shoes. And, then, some deep memories of your fathering as I grew up really helped. It suddenly occurred to me that those memories could not be erased by the shock of learning you were a homosexual. For me, you're the same father I had from the beginning. You've always made me proud to be your son, and that will continue. We must all, you, Mom and me, we must all let it be and move on."

Adam nodded. George noticed how exhausted he looked.

"I know you're tired. I won't be long. But I love you so much, and here's some reasons why. Your support. Constant. Allowing me to wander, drift, explore, jump into the bramble patch, figure out my own take on religion. Your acceptance. Complete. Always ready with a word of advice, but never pushy about delivery. The incredibly wide range of knowledge you shared with me. Generously and all the time. And, finally, you never insisted I call you 'Father.' Hang on, Dad. I expect to be back to see you again soon."

Adam listened, his mind wading into murky waters of guilt over his many nights at the office instead of being home, parenting George with Liz. Here was a guilt that infected his view of being a father, a guilt he couldn't cure but couldn't confess to George and apologize for either.

At the door, George asked Bernie if there were any promising drugs to be had.

"I'm trying to stay on top of that. As far as I know, nothing yet has done the job. But I'm checking all the time. Doctors have some confidence they will develop something that works, but they can't say how soon, and, sadly, we don't have all the time in the world. It's a race, AIDS against science."

George grabbed Bernie's arm, pulled him in, hugged tight. For a second time within the hour, he shed tears.

"You've not tested positive, have you?"

"No, I'm okay."

"That's important. Someone has to stay around to tell the story. I'm so thankful Dad's got you with him. Goodbye for now."

In the months following the concert, Adam's condition worsened. He stayed in bed through the morning hours, rising for a bird-like lunch, then reading, going out to walk a block or two, and often returning to bed. Reading tired him.

"I'm going to beat this monster, Bernie. Remember what the Doc said about attitude. I'm going to live because I want to. I want to so much. And, by the way, the firm's going to continue my draw. At least for the foreseeable future, regardless. How's that for class?"

By the beginning of November, with writing on the wall in capital letters, Adam acknowledged to Bernie a decline in his condition. By then, his mobility was limited to a wheelchair. One clear, brisk and cloudless fall morning, Adam asked Bernie to take him to Fahnestock Park, in Carmel, a place he had started visiting as a kid and continued to use as his hiking site of choice through the years. Too often to count, he had brought Liz and George to Fahnestock for a day of hiking the trails with sandwiches nestled in backpacks for lunch.

"We can try the Clove Creek Trail. It should work for my chariot."

"Sounds like fun. I'll bring a whip."

Bernie helped Adam put on a warm fleece coat and then wrapped him in a long wool scarf and pulled down on his head his favorite tasseled wool hat. They reached the Park in early afternoon. Bernie opened up the wheelchair and set off, pushing Adam along the trail. Late summer and early fall rains had kept the ground moist, the tree roots nourished. On both sides of the trail, the late colors of autumn dazzled, while a brook filled to capacity gurgled its way down the gentle hill that Bernie was walking up, the wheelchair held firm ahead of him. Leaves covered the trail and fell on and around them as they moved slowly along the trail.

Awakening from a brief slumber to the blaze of color around him, Adam imagined he had passed though those pearly gates. "Where are we?" he croaked, his voice, like other bodily elements, not what it used to be.

"We're in Fahnestock, where you asked me to bring you. Just look at these yellows. They bring out the poet in me: feathered by wind, filtered with sun. At moments like this, I can imagine the thrill of being a great landscape painter."

"Bernie, being a city kid, you may not know these trees. I'll help you, if you don't mind my raven's whisper. So, those yellows tinged with red are red maples. And the brown leaves with yellow to green edging, one could call it chartreuse, those are beech trees."

"Brown's too simple a color to describe the beech, Adam. How about bronze?"

"Okay. Better. And then there's the various scarlets of the dogwoods, the high bush blueberry and the blackberries. And look at the small white pines, yellowing needles under the green. I've always loved the way their green needles shimmer in the sun. It's a stunning contrast. If this trail doesn't lead to heaven, it can't be far off."

They continued along the trail, absorbing the colors. Bernie sensed the tree lesson was a sign that Adam wanted in some way to be in charge again.

"Bernie, do you remember the night we met? We literally bumped into each other. Then the bar, beers, talk. The electricity we felt."

"I recall it all. Just as you put it. A night to remember. Especially now, as we roll along."

"I think of Frost's road not taken. You know, making all the difference. Well, perhaps it's not a stretch to say we've both lived it."

In time, Adam began to cough. Bernie saw he was shivering and wrapped his long scarf around and around Adam's neck.

"I think we've seen enough. There's a chill in the air. I don't want you to catch cold." They were motionless, silent for a minute, both in pain from the thought of the horrible illness slowly destroying Adam, the one that was wrenching his life away from all those who loved him.

Bernie swung the chariot around and followed the trail back to their car. The scene had changed but was no less spectacular. Same arboreal colors but now backlighted, offering an entirely different look.

Like a sled gliding downhill, slowly at first, then gathering speed, Adam's disease accelerated after the concert. It was as if, through a determined act of will, Adam had kept AIDS at bay until he had finished singing *Life and Death in the Time of AIDS,* only to have it surge again when the concert was over.

Bernie held him as Adam's life ebbed away. Adam's mind seemed riveted to Dylan Thomas' *Fern Hill,* groping for words. Finally, he remembered the last stanza.

"Oh as I was young and easy in the mercy of his means,

Time held me green and dying though I sang through my chains like the sea."

He didn't suffer in the closing minutes. Bernie gathered to himself all the suffering in the room as he held Adam in his arms, watching his breathing soften and then cease. He felt his heart break with the knowledge that his partner was dead.

⚬ි⚬

Over the past year, Liz had made a list of things to do when, and if, Adam succumbed to AIDS. Among the items, was concern over the obit she knew his law firm would prepare. Soon after learning of Adam's death, she called Charlie Pott to express interest in seeing what the firm proposed to say.

"I'll get you the draft as soon as it's ready."

A first draft was written by the office publicist.

The lead: "Adam Zopher Hudson, a partner in the law firm of Bundy, Rogers & Freund in Manhattan, died of pancreatic failure, a complication of AIDS, yesterday at New York University Hospital."

Robert Russell, the partner responsible for Mitsubishi, got a copy and objected strenuously. He claimed the Japanese would be shocked that Adam, who had done much legal work for that client and was much admired by them, was a homosexual. He believed the shock would be enough to cause them to drop the firm.

Charlie couldn't believe his partner's opinion. He had sent the draft to Liz. Now, he called her to see what she thought.

"It's just right," she told him. "Thanks for sharing."

Charlie decided to tell Liz of Robert Russell's objection.

"That's really not what Adam would have wanted. He was out of the closet, at peace with his sexuality. I'm sure he would want the reason for his death—after all he was still young and vigorous—explained in the notice."

Charlie remembered Robert's objection to taking on the pro bono case against New York's sodomy law. He had been at that partners' lunch and watched Adam during the debate. Armed now with Liz's unqualified support for the draft, he took the matter to George Banville, asking Robert Russell to join him.

Faced with Charlie's insistence, based not just on the truth but on the desire of Adam's wife and her confident opinion of what Adam, himself, would have wanted, Robert backed down. George Banville closed out the discussion.

"As between clients and partners, partners come first."

The firm was pleased to learn from its client, Mitsubishi, that Adam's loss to the firm was seen as a loss to the client as well, with the effect of tightening the bond between them.

Adam had died on August 20, 1990. Soon after, Liz and Bernie sat down over lunch at the Brasserie, knowing well that it was a work-night haunt of Adam's when detained at the office. Their purpose was to plan a memorial service for Adam, to be held at the Empire. They ordered the famed onion soup and burgers. Remembering Adam's love for this bistro, the memory of him was, for both of them, acute.

"Liz, I feel this a most bitter-sweet moment. Bitter, in thinking, for the umpteenth time the unfairness of what we are here forced to accept. But it's sweet in allowing me to join you in planning the celebration."

"He was going to enjoy a long life, for sure, if it hadn't been cheated by AIDS. So, let me report where things stand. I called Byard and asked him for two favors in honor of Adam: One, to arrange for the memorial service at his club, and two, knowing he's a pianist, to play at the memorial. I suggested an introduction to the event, playing a Debussy piece favored by Adam, *Reflets dans l'eau*, and then, in conclusion, another favorite of Adam's, Bach's

Prelude and Fugue in E flat minor. Byard said he was honored. What do you think?"

"I'm sure Byard is really pleased to be part of this. So, don't we need someone to welcome the guests. How about George?"

"Yes, if he'll do it. And it needn't be a speech. Short and to the point."

"Liz, will you speak?"

"I've thought about that. The answer's yes, but only if you speak too."

"You know I would. Should we have someone from the Bundy firm?"

"Definitely. I think Charlie is the right one. One of Adam's closest and for me one of the most sensitive and kind sort of guy I know." Looking at Bernie with a twinkle in her eye, she added: "After you."

"And now, we come to the question of the Father. Should you ask him to speak?"

Liz examined Bernie's face—was he kidding? "I don't think we want him present at what everyone *except* him will view as a celebration of a life well lived. Remember, he refused to come to the concert, and even blocked Hannah from attending."

"But doesn't he have to be invited? And Hannah? Whether they show up will be their choice, not ours. We won't ask him to speak. That would be too much."

"Agreed."

" So, returning to us, we don't want to cover the same stuff. Do you have some thoughts on what you might say?"

"Yes, I've been thinking about that a lot lately. I'll begin by saying that all his life, Adam lived for his father's recognition and approval. In the end, he died without it. And no man deserved recognition and approval more. I've considered whether I could say this with the old man present. And, yes, I want to say it, whether in front of Dwight or not. I'll say that Adam carried with him a profound sadness that he would never be accepted as a whole person by his father and even by some of his colleagues. Perhaps even by himself, although I believe he thought he'd reached a wholeness, only tragically to have that wholeness cut short. And how about you?"

"I think I'll speak of the freedom—a blossoming, one could call it—Adam experienced after you encouraged him to separate in order that he might live as the man he was—a gay man in need of friendship and support in a gay culture in which he could discover a group of his peers. The blooming could be seen on various roads. He took up cooking, and quickly mastered it. He returned to choral singing and helped design that wonderful AIDS program. He renewed his love of photography. He became a man at ease, relaxed, experimental, freed from the need to get things right the first time. My love for the guy grew with every turn in the road."

"That's it, exactly. At first, he tip-toed out of the closet. But, as later he put it to me, 'the more open I became, the more confident I became about my sexuality and the easier it was to be out.' He was able to settle into himself with comfort and enjoy his new gay friends, and know, however bafflingly ambiguous his life has been, he was now on the right pathway. The sorrow—the deep sorrow—is that he didn't have enough time to realize the promise, to experience and, yes, to celebrate the man he was becoming."

"And one more thing, Liz. If you approve, that is. I'd like to present George with my portrait of his father, the one I did soon after we started living together, when he appeared to be at the peak of robust health."

"Agreed. The best way possible to end the proceeding."

When the memorial service was booked and the program planned, Liz called Hannah. And later that afternoon, she called George. She ran through the plan with each of them. George said he'd be happy to kick things off.

When Wright came home, Hannah reported to him on Liz's call.

"I don't plan on attending. It would be too painful. I haven't even been asked to speak. I wouldn't want to; I'd decline if asked."

"I'll be there for both of us," Hannah said.

❦

On the night before the memorial, Hannah had trouble sleeping. Around two, she took a mild sleeping pill, which soon put her into a deep sleep. In the morning, with a wince, and a deep emptiness in her belly, she recalled a dream. She was in a sculptor's workshop. A large, nearly finished sculpture of a young man, naked, was in the middle of the room. The sculptor, who she thought might be her husband, was working on the marble, chisel and mallet in hand. She saw he was frustrated by the marble where the chisel was being applied. It wasn't responding to the hammer as the sculptor wished. He increased the strength of the hammer's blow that he sent through the chisel to the marble body. It was a mighty blow and broke the sculpture to pieces.

❦

Hannah returned from the memorial to find Wright standing at the door, obviously having awaited her and anxious for a report. They sat in the living room, over tea, and she described the service. Hannah saw how hard it was for Wright, wanting desperately to know all the details, wanting to know if he was missed, and then, flipping the story, not wanting to hear more. Hannah's account caused him to become aware of how Liz and George might view his role in the shaping of Adam's life. And how Hannah weighed his influence. Indeed, how others too, those who knew the family well. As he had always been able to do in matters of self-defense, he used his well-disciplined mind to try to rid himself of these ugly thoughts.

"How did it end?" Wright asked, still overcome with curiosity.

"Bernie delivered the 'benediction' by just quoting Walt Whitman. I wrote it down:

> 'I have said that the soul is not more than the body,
>
> And I have said that the body is not more than the soul,
>
> And nothing, not God, is greater to one than one's self is,

And whoever walks a furlong without sympathy walks to his own funeral drest in his shroud…' "

Looking up from her notes at Wright's ashen face, Hannah knew he was struggling. And she couldn't think of any way to help, except possibly to put one final point on her story.

"It was a beautiful event. What came shining through all that was said, all the music that was played, all the vibes pulsing in the room, was that our son was a man of many parts, a man beloved by many friends, a man of high accomplishment. Yes, and a man of kindness and generosity of spirit. He should make us both very proud."

THE END

✑ ACKNOWLEDGMENTS ✑

This novel is derived from experiences of a lifetime and friendships forged both socially and professionally, braided together to form a narrative nearly unrecognizable if examined through its parts.

Out of the Whirlwind is the story of a man's life, looked at both inside and out, a life of stress and strength. He faced handicaps that hardened to impede growth until finally overcome. He possessed immense talent that faced many tests without faltering, and a personal identity shaped slowly and in pain until accepted late in a life cut short before its time.

I enjoyed, and will always remain most grateful for, the serious encouragement from those who knew what I was trying to accomplish, including most importantly Bruce Haims, Tom Kelly, Ralph Arditi, Erik Kulleseid and Tom Wright, each of whom went beyond encouraging sounds to actually reading the manuscript with attention and thoughtful comment. And, to this list, although they did not read the manuscript, I must add Charles Ellis, Clark Remington and Doug Gruenau, whose understanding and encouragement was, in each case, important ballast.

I was fortunate to have other readers as well, whose comments were unfailingly to the point and most helpful. They include James Engell, Franny Taliaferro, Susan Carey, Dominique Browning, Tim Wirth and Kim Townsend.

As with my previous novels, I turned to Karen Shepard, Professor at Williams College and author of many distinguished works of fiction, for a careful reading and reaction to the manuscript, which resulted in a range of improvements, large and small. My wife, Clara, and my daughter, Katie, both contributed ideas to improve the manuscript, ideas for which I am most grateful.

I also wish here to acknowledge with appreciation the art work found on the cover. The artist, Noah Saterstrom, is a highly talented resident of Nashville. In addition, I acknowledge the excellent layout work and production talents of Tony Bonds, who, operating under the title "Golden Ratio Book Design," assisted in this novel as he did in *Chains Across the River*.